A book of wisdo

Nikhil Parekh

Proverse Hong Kong

2022

SEEKING SOLACE, a collection of poetry in free verse, encompasses and glorifies one of the most quintessential of human needs, self help. The poet, Nikhil Parekh, takes the view that in the current world scenario—disastrously fraught with terrorism, war, prejudice, unemployment of various kinds—if you want to help others, you must first help yourself. This is because positivity can diffuse efficaciously from a soul which is harmonious in itself with the spirit of victorious existence. Various of the poems embodied in this collection earnestly aim at applying the balm of uninhibited hope, optimistic enlightenment, righteous empowerment, and self-friendship upon humanity.

NIKHIL PAREKH (born 27August 1977) is the author of 47 books of poetry. With his wife, his daughters, Kavya and Kyra, his mother and father and sister, he lives in the city of Ahmedabad, Gujarat State, on the west coast of India. He has travelled to London, UK, and Switzerland. As recorded by the *Limca Book of Records India* (an annual Indian publication similar to what is now known as *Guinness World Records*), he is a ten-time National Record holder for his poetry.

**NIKHIL PAREKH'S "SEEKING SOLACE"
IS THE WINNER
OF A PROVERSE PUBLICATION PRIZE 2021**

SEEKING SOLACE

By

Nikhil Parekh

*A Book of Wisdom and Delight
for the Modern World*

Proverse Hong Kong

Seeking Solace
By Nikhil Parekh
First published in Hong Kong
by Proverse Hong Kong,
under sole and exclusive right and licence,
17 November 2022
Paperback: ISBN 13: 978-988-8492-58-9
E-book: ISBN 13: 978-988-8492-59-6

Distribution (Hong Kong and worldwide)
The Chinese University of Hong Kong Press,
The Chinese University of Hong Kong,
Shatin, New Territories, Hong Kong SAR.
Email: cup@cuhk.edu.hk; Web: www.cup.cuhk.edu.hk
Distribution (United Kingdom)
Stephen Inman, Worcester, UK.
Enquiries to Proverse Hong Kong
P.O. Box 259, Tung Chung Post Office,
Lantau, NT, Hong Kong SAR, China.
Email: proverse@netvigator.com;
Web: www.proversepublishing.com

Cover image: "Five Mandalas of the Vajravali system", c. 1430,
public domain. Downloaded from wikimedia commons.

British Library Cataloguing in Publication Data
A catalogue record for the first paperback edition
is available from the British Library

SEEKING SOLACE

Nikhil Parekh

Contents

Preface

In the face of human suffering, political skulduggery, and the universal problem of evil, Voltaire's advice about cultivating our own garden seems to be the only escapist conclusion to which he can arrive, both philosophically and practically. At first view, Nikhil Parekh's *Seeking Solace* seems to rest on the same fertile ground as that found in the conclusion of *Candide—or Optimism*. But there is a fundamental and dramatic difference between the two works. In light of the catalogue of disasters and crises Pangloss faces throughout the book, Voltaire's ultimate agricultural conclusion feels rather weak, almost apologetic. Pangloss' own name suggests sterile volubility since his name, translated from the Greek, means "all tongue". Voltaire's is a satire on philosophical optimism, while Parekh's poetry is as far from satire as you can go; a shameless celebration of what I would call extreme psycho-artistic optimism.

Parekh allows for the severe trials that beset us all, describing them with forthright honesty: for example, suicide in 'Embrace unconquerable life', or hopelessness in 'Life without a purpose', or physical decline in 'If I had closed my breath yesterday'. But in these trials, and many other crises which weave in and out of almost every poem, he allows his potent persona—the irrepressible Self— to take charge and triumph. He is to poetry what superheroes are to Marvel and DC Comics. The poet is never evasive: in fact, the very opposite. For example, in 'Victory shall forever be' he presents a catalogue of the truly obscene: "Every maelstrom of unendingly truculent misery", "Every corpse of ghoulishly ungainly torture", "giving uninhibited liberty to the devil to do whatever he can", and

"Every hell of preposterously raunchy sin"—the list could go on in that poem alone. So how does he counteract the multitude of hideously negative images that he allows into his verse in this volume? One way is the sheer energy of his speaking persona, the shameless "I" who presents throughout the work through an almost unrestrained and wilful variety of versions of the heroic, omnipotent Self. His repetitive lines and their tight stanzaic forms encourage the kind of reading that is almost chant-like, with rhythmic runs that refuse defeat.

Here is no quiet, introspective poetic musing, but a chanting in-your-face celebrant of Self. He even out-Whitmans Walt Whitman: "You might say that the letter 'I' singularly by itself was... sinfully plundering selfishness..." But unless and until "you unflinchingly worship the 'I'... How can you ever dream of lovingly and wholesomely embracing others?"

In this collection you cannot avoid the inescapable vocal and dramatic energy—it trumpets itself with a complete absence of shame or guilt, and will use bathos, pathos, unapologetic sentimentality or even strident melodrama to reach its end. To call his verse bold is an understatement, as it works sincerely and furiously towards a point of acceptance in the final poem: to emerge "victorious from behind my vicious outburst of gloom" and to reveal "my true identity... without the slightest fear."

Parekh's poetic energy, his raw honesty and his highly unique and strident, individual style make it hard not to get caught up in his refusal to bow to the various forms of cynicism which plague our current age—no matter how bad they are. He has to swim a lot in a rising flood of pain, doubt and contempt (and does so furiously) but he point-blank refuses to be drowned, or to escape, as Voltaire's *Candide* suggests one should, to a gardening project that could easily be dismissed as mild, solipsistic escapism.

George Watt
Adelaide 15 June 2022

Nikhil Parekh, Seeking Solace

SEEKING SOLACE

Poems of delight and wisdom
for the modern world

Good Morning, Sunshine

Good Morning, Sunshine; thank you for filtering
stringently through my dingily dilapidated window;
embedding optimistic rays of hope in my life,

Good Morning, Cuckoo; thank you for waking up my
gloomy sleep with your poignantly austere sounds,

Good Morning, Grass; thank you for rejuvenating my
dreary soles, as I trespassed on your voluptuous
carpet, with your magnificent sheath of dew-drops
tickling my skin to unprecedented limits

Good Morning, delectable pet; thank you for
clambering up my bed, awakening me with a pleasant
jolt, as you flapped your slippery tongue over my
rubicund cheeks

Good Morning, Shirt; thank you for imparting me
with compassionate warmth, as I swung you over my
naked chest the instant I broke my reverie

Good Morning, Wife; thank you for providing me
your mesmerizing shoulders to rest upon in times of
the treacherous night

Good Morning, Air; thank you for so celestially
wafting into my nostrils, seductively caressing my
mass of unruly hair to transit me higher than the
heavens

Good Morning, Lotus; thank you for spreading your
ingratiatingly pink petals into full bloom, inundating
my solitary life with astronomical happiness

Good Morning, Tea; thank you for profoundly
reinvigorating my diminishing breath, fomenting me
to walk briskly forward with untamed exhilaration

Good Morning, Water; thank you for pacifying my
thirst, inevitably providing me those few sips of liquid
to quench the scorched chords of my throat, the
second I detached from horrendous dreams

Good Morning, Soap; thank you for providing me
tons of enamoring foam, which metamorphosed my
bedraggled person into one of stupendously
distinguished authority

Good Morning, National Flag; thank you for fluttering
so handsomely in the atmosphere, propelling the spirit
of patriotism to escalate unsurpassably in my veins,
the second I nimbly opened my eyelids at dawn

Good Morning, Soil; thank you for impregnably
holding the foundations of my dwelling, harboring my
inconspicuous demeanor while I slept like a new born
infant in the perilous night

Good Morning, Apple; thank you for providing me
that incredulously quick bite before I eloped for the
office, prepared to kick on with my schedule for the
acrimoniously monotonous day

Good Morning, Mother; thank you for silently
creeping up beside me when I was in bouts of
thunderously sound sleep, gently caressing my hair;
embodying my shivering countenance with a sweater
you had specially knitted for me in the day

Good Morning, Tree; thank you for generating appeasing draughts of wind which diffused through my window as the Sun crept up in the sky, making me feel that I was indispensably alive

Good Morning, Breath; thank you for blissfully circulating through my lungs, enveloping me with the tenacity to divinely pass the gruesomely precarious night

And Good Morning, World; thank you for granting me the right to exist harmoniously amongst you, walk shoulder to shoulder with your blessed grace in every aspect of exuberant life.

Let's pray for love

Let's pray with our fingers invincibly clasped for
UNITY, for a wave of perpetual solidarity to descend
charismatically all over the monotonously bedraggled
planet

Let's pray with untamed fires blazing in our eyes for
PROSPERITY, uplifting all those tottering with
relentlessly acrid pain to the ultimate realms of
bountifully enamoring paradise

Let's pray with divine obeisance enshrouding our
souls for HARMONY, for the winds of celestial
symbiosis to emphatically deluge every treacherously
shattered life

Let's pray with Herculean energy in our shoulders for
RESILIENCE, for an unflinching attitude to confront
the mightiest of disasters for all those miserably
shivering and pathetically deprived

Let's pray with overwhelming bliss enveloping our
senses for PEACE—the immortal cloud of
rhapsodically contented happiness—to shower its
heavenly blessings upon the rich, poor, and
devastatingly orphaned, alike,

Let's pray with insatiable nostalgia in our blood for
INNOCENCE, for all lecherously satanic life loitering
insidiously upon this boundless Universe to
metamorphose into a garland of Godly childhood

Let's pray with unrelenting ardor in our conscience for
TRUTH, for the wholesome overshadowing of satanic
evil on the trajectory of this enchanting planet by the
threads of unassailable righteousness

Let's pray with stupendous belief in our veins for
EQUALITY, the uninhibited virtue of compassion
entrenching different souls pathetically staggering, for
volatile trace of indispensably vital life

Let's pray with insurmountable glory in our voice for
FREEDOM -- an irrefutably unconquerable spirit -- to
unequivocally exist amidst the diabolically tyrannical
lingering reflections of the bizarre devil

Let's pray with unparalleled eloquence in our
impoverished visage for BEAUTY -- an
unsurpassably redolent flower of humanity – to engulf
all webs of maliciously manipulative and rotten
prejudice

Let's pray with an unprecedented shimmer upon our
lips for BROTHERHOOD, for all disastrously
orphaned destitute, coalesced synergistically together,
to handsomely
evolve into a wonderfully endowing and majestically
sparkling tomorrow

Let's pray with indefatigable strength in our palms for
SYMBIOSIS, for a profound mélangeing of all tribes,
castes and religions on this fathomless planet, to scrap
the very essence of the ignominiously rebuking devil
from its worthlessly non-existent rudiments

Let's pray with incomprehensibly melodious charisma
in our eyelashes for SOLITUDE, for an irrevocably
unshakable tenacity to exist in a land of supreme
pacification and heavenly joy descending torrentially
from all sides

Let's pray with unfazed belonging in each pore of our skin for WISDOM, for the bells of an invincible triumph over despicably despairing sadness, ringing loud and poignantly stringent through the frigid cocoons of a lackadaisical atmosphere

Let's pray with joyously swirling desire in our blood for BENEVOLENCE, for an evergreen carpet of marvelously omnipotent showering upon all those entities murderously encompassed by gruesomely ominous hopelessness

Let's pray with magnificent majesty in our shadows for TOGETHERNESS -- a spirit of pricelessly augmenting passion -- to wholeheartedly circumvent all those miserably divested of their revered mates in penalizing life

Let's pray with altruistic faith in our innocuously glorious countenances for SUCCESS; the pearls of sagaciously benign wisdom to perpetuate a serenely satisfying chapter of existence; in the lives of those uncouthly engulfed by savage blood; indiscriminate crime and horrific lies

Let's pray with an intransigently sacrosanct propensity in our breaths for LIFE; a prolific dissemination of its fathomlessly fabulous repertoire of spell-binding forms and its perpetually Omnipotent spirit to philanthropically survive, reigning supreme in every birth it was bequeathed from the Almighty Lord

And let's pray with an immortally royal fervor in our hearts for LOVE, its miraculously healing touch proving the ultimate panacea for harmoniously surviving and blossoming into wonderful lives.

Happiness

Happiness is in sighting the stars that glow
exuberantly in the sky, profoundly illuminating the
treachery of the murderously satanic night

Happiness is in gallivanting freely through the
meandering hills, letting the breeze from the scarlet
horizons tickle you profusely till the ultimate spine
down your nape

Happiness is in benevolently donating, witnessing an
invincible smile light up on impoverished faces
submerged in a cloud of derogatory sadness

Happiness is in bouncing ebulliently on the lap of
your sacrosanct mother, completely surrendering your
immaculate identity in her magnanimously divine
swirl

Happiness is in inundating barren mountains of canvas
with resplendent color, assimilating the mesmerizing
beauty of the planet in astoundingly vivacious shapes
and forms

Happiness is in inhaling the fragrance of soil and
ravishing rose, being enthralled till times beyond
eternity as you roll full throttle on the seductive
carpets of lush green grass

Happiness is in whistling melodiously across the
gorgeously fathomless gorge, letting the mystical
volley of exotic echoes encompass your boisterous
visage from all sides

Happiness is in floating uninhibitedly in the placid
lakes, letting the animated festoon of incredible
dolphins leap ecstatically by your side

Happiness is in dancing vibrantly with the impeccable
fairies, profoundly relishing the marvelously pearly
rays of shimmering moon on each cranny of your
drearily devastated skin

Happiness is in fighting unrelentingly for the ultimate
essence of truth disseminating its Godly virtue to the
farthest and remotest corner of this gigantic earth

Happiness is in discovering an insurmountable
battalion of newness every unfurling second of the
day, bemusing the gloomy cells of your mind with
unprecedented intrigue

Happiness is in harboring all whom you encountered
in their times of despairing distress, embracing them
equally with the candle of humanity flaming profusely
in your soul

Happiness is in dedicating your life to the service of
the deprived, persevering as the richest man on this
Universe, while your fellow comrades exist
under the stupendously magnificent glory of royal
Sunshine

Happiness is in commencing each day as a fresh
chapter of life, intrepidly transcending over the
miseries of the dolorous past, filtering blissful
pouches of space to survive

Happiness is in breathing for your cherished mission
till time immemorial, following the innermost voices
of your passionately throbbing heart, even as the
uncouth world outside lambasted you insidiously from
all sides

Happiness is in leading life higher than the clouds, affording the same to your tangible friends till the moment the Almighty Lord wants you to wander and survive

Happiness is in considering yourself to be just a whisker of God's infinite Creation and yet feeling the most endowed molecule alive

Happiness is in caring, Happiness is in sharing, Happiness is in unity, Happiness is in beauty, Happiness is in immortal love -- and most importantly true -- Happiness is in the chapter called LIFE.

After every devil there is God

After every gruesome night, there rises the brilliant day, with the sun dazzling profoundly in the sky

After every storm, there descends a celestial stillness, which impregnates the ambience with unprecedented peace

After every anecdote of horrendous pain, there is unparalleled joy, with signs of triumph and ecstatic jubilation

After every turbulent wave that rises to astronomical heights in the sea, there is sedate water, which languidly floats towards the shores

After every savage slope of the treacherous mountain there lies the sweet valley, inundating the atmosphere with its mysticism and charm

After every whirlwind accompanied with gusty currents of wild wind, there is plain dust, which meekly settles on all quarters of exposed surface

After every bout of epidemic fever, there lies immunity to infection compounded with sporadic spurts of robust health

After every spell of frozen winter, there lies enchanting summer, with infinite springs of molten liquid cascading down

After every winding road aligned with a plethora of acerbic barricades, there lies the impeccably straight lane
After every shrub of the acrimoniously thorny cactus, lies the crimson and fragrant rose

After every ominous black cloud ready to pelt down
thunderous rain, there lies the crystal blue network of
clear sky

After every island of adulterated fertilizer crop, there
lies the innocuous and tall tree

After every dark space in the colossal cosmos, there
lies the resplendently twinkling star

After every little inconspicuous mosquito hovering in
the air, there lie infinite molecules of golden sawdust
shimmering in the sunshine

After every hell existing on this globe, there lies the
mesmerizing ocean of paradise

After every incidence of miserable failure in life, there
lie loads of unsurpassable success

After every lie spoken with blatant audacity, there lies
the perpetual truth

After every horrendous dream throughout the course
of the night, there lies the serene morning

After every parable of overwhelming hatred, there lies
immortal and unbiased love

And after every diabolical demon confronted on this
earth, there lies the omniscient CREATOR.

Perpetual privilege

The most irrefutably perpetual privilege for the
mother was to feed her baby with gallons of
uninhibitedly sacrosanct milk

The most irrefutably perpetual privilege for the flower
was to disseminate its spell-binding fragrance to those
quarters of the earth despondently besieged with
horrifically despicable doom and unsurpassable
gloominess

The most irrefutably perpetual privilege for the star
was to inundate the complexion of the drearily
exhausted night with unprecedented whirlwinds of
captivating mysticism

The most irrefutably perpetual privilege for the clouds
was to incessantly shower its globules of celestial
water upon miserably slithering cocoons of ominously
entrenched and overwhelmingly parched soil

The most irrefutably perpetual privilege for the lips
was to trigger maelstroms of invincible passion in
fatigued bodies treacherously engrossed in digging
their very own graves

The most irrefutably perpetual privilege for the singer
was to divinely pacify its colossal battalion of
penuriously staggering audiences with
overwhelmingly melodious music

The most irrefutably perpetual privilege for the
dwelling was to impregnably grant shelter to the
insidiously deprived, heal the most lecherously
devastated senses with the ointment of compassionate
sharing

The most irrefutably perpetual privilege for the pen
was to emboss exquisite lines of majestic artistry upon
boundlessly barren sheets of paper, weave an
unsurpassable trail of magical enigma with scarlet ink
incarcerated in its congenial belly

The most irrefutably perpetual privilege for the tree
was to bequeath an incomprehensible tunnel of
bountiful fruits upon organisms remorsefully curled
in famished malice

The most irrefutably perpetual privilege for the sheep
was to unequivocally bestow its amiably cozy tufts of
wool, engulfing all those malevolently orphaned in
blankets of poignantly swirling warmth

The most irrefutably perpetual privilege for the
newspaper was to ubiquitously keep its readers
apprised about the latest global happenings unveiling
timelessly and all round the clock

The most irrefutably perpetual privilege for the
mountain was to unrelentingly tower above all on the
trajectory of this mesmerizing Universe, undisputedly
be the first one to kiss the golden Sun as it
marvelously blazed through azure carpets of blissful
sky

The most irrefutably perpetual privilege for the soldier
was to free his immaculately revered motherland from
the clutches of insatiably murderous diabolism

The most irrefutably perpetual privilege for the arrow
was to strike its barbarically savage target head-on,
even before it could dare to bat an infinitesimally
single eyelid

The most irrefutably perpetual privilege for the stream
was to celestially placate the thirst of countless bleary-
eyed travelers, magnificently rejuvenate every
element of their bedraggled senses, propelling them to
philanthropically triumph in life

The most irrefutably perpetual privilege for the doctor
was to benevolently cure his patients of their most
inexplicable ailments and despairing pain, scrap
stinking debilitation and disease from its very non-
existent roots entirely from the trajectory of
this eternally infinite planet

The most irrefutably perpetual privilege for the saint
was to ensure that his unending entrenchment of
diligent disciples perennially disseminated the
immortal essence of peace, love and sagacious truth to
even the most remotest corners of this mammoth
Universe

The most irrefutably perpetual privilege for the body
was to unsurpassably accomplish its optimum quota
of benevolent deeds and desire in the tenure of its
transiently stipulated life, affording the same to its
fellow compatriots in irascible distress

And the most irrefutably perpetual privilege for the
heart was to immortally shower upon its pricelessly
vivacious beats of love on every soil where it
handsomely gallivanted, instilling the most supremely
royal gift of the Almighty Lord in every entity existing
and also in those yet to evolve into fragrantly vibrant
life.

Any form of life was better than death

I felt like committing suicide there and then,
every time I saw countless haplessly orphaned
children being viciously kicked into dustbins of
malice for ostensibly no reason or rhyme

I felt like committing suicide there and then,
every time I saw the pricelessly innocuous female
fetus being brutally assassinated and aborted right in
the very depths of the unassailably godly womb

I felt like committing suicide there and then,
every time I saw heartlessly cold-blooded men
ruthlessly felling innumerable trees, using its blessed
branches, trunk and roots for evolving lifelessly
wastrel commodities

I felt like committing suicide there and then,
every time I saw demonically manipulating politicians
weigh the very essence of unconquerably righteous
life in terms of wantonly decrepit currency coin

I felt like committing suicide there and then,
every time I saw innocent under-age girls being
brutally raped by the diabolically idiosyncratic
perversions of sadistic men

I felt like committing suicide there and then,
every time I saw boundless wives and children
reduced to a cadaverous carcass, as the man of the
family simply refrained to budge an inch to earn,
cannibalistically guzzling the last drop of wine and
vittles to be found on planet earth

I felt like committing suicide there and then,
every time I saw beautifully fructifying wildlife being
emotionlessly beheaded, just in order to become the
exuberant delicacy of the already replenished palette

I felt like committing suicide there and then,
every time I saw robustly ebullient organisms doing
nothing but just endlessly gazing at the fathomless
sky, nonsensically proclaiming that their destiny
would one day and eventually take them to the
absolute epitome of cloud nine

I felt like committing suicide there and then,
every time I saw one man derogatorily slaving and
slavering for another man, whereas the Omnipotent
Creator had created all symbiotically equal in the first
place

I felt like committing suicide there and then,
every time I saw millions of innocent beings
indiscriminately butchered in the wrath and aftermath
of barbarously thwarting bombardment and war

I felt like committing suicide there and then,
every time I saw satanic terrorists launch an
inconsolably pulverizing assault on one particular
fraternity of mankind in the name of sacrifice to the
Omnipresent Lord

I felt like committing suicide there and then,
every time I saw hordes of people blind-foldedly
offering their last ounce of wealth to the Omnipotent
deity of the Lord, who in the first place owned every
speck of the unending Universe and who wanted them
to benevolently donate the same to all suffering living
kind instead

I felt like committing suicide there and then,
every time I saw school-going girls and boys begging
hoarsely on the obdurately chauvinistic streets, with
their parents abhorrently using them to tickle the soft
hearts of opulent society

I felt like committing suicide there and then,
every time I saw women of all ages, right from the age
of my daughter to sister to mother, tawdrily selling
their flesh to hedonistically dastardly men just for
securing those two quintessential morsels of food

I felt like committing suicide there and then,
every time I saw limitless numbers dying unattended
on the freezing streets because of unforgivably ghastly
corruption viciously infiltrating in every echelon of
the government and society

I felt like committing suicide there and then,
every time I saw the most perpetually faithful of
lovers salaciously separate like a miserably broken
leaf at the tiniest objection from the sanctimoniously
turgid society

I felt like committing suicide there and then,
every time I saw selfishly shriveled man praying to
God solely for impregnating his lungs with countless
breaths, instead of immortally sharing the same in
perfect symbiosis with endless numbers of his own
kind

But when I was actually committing suicide, I felt that
any form of life was better than death as I approached
my very last breath. For if at all I could endeavor my
very best to ameliorate every fraternity of estranged
living-kind, then by the grace of God it could be done
only while in undefeated life and not the slightest after
stonily gory death.

Your best company is you yourself

Nobody on earth could eat for you other than you yourself, in order to blissfully mollify all those thwarting pangs of hunger, which if left untreated would render you soon into a brutally disheveled corpse

Nobody on earth could walk for you other than you yourself, in order to magically ease the wretchedly restless energy circumventing your bored feet, as they fervently stamp the earth and kiss the oncoming exuberant draughts of air

Nobody on earth could talk for you other than you yourself, in order to give voice to all those quintessentially simmering thoughts, inevitably wanting to be poured outside the barren chest

Nobody on earth could watch a film for you other than you yourself, in order to fantasize and emotively feel beyond realms of the extraordinary, which mundane life otherwise never allowed you to dare

Nobody on earth could smile for you other than you yourself, in order to feel bounteously happy from the innermost realms of your soul, for living every moment in the true pulse of bountifully enamoring life

Nobody on earth could sleep for you other than you yourself, in order to render every cranny of your drearily impoverished countenance that heavenly respite and enable you to gallop once again towards effulgent righteousness the instant you opened your eyes

Nobody on earth could dream for you other than you yourself, in order to visualize the most inscrutable enigmas and colors on this Universe, and then express them in myriad forms like poetry, paintings, music by the grace of the Almighty Lord

Nobody on earth could wash for you other than you yourself, in order to be bereft of all incorrigibly adulterated grease, and then emerge into dazzling fresh sunshine to unabashedly enjoy for a countless more lifetimes

Nobody on earth could sing for you other than you yourself, in order to perpetuate obsolete wisps of fleeting atmosphere, with the passionate fire of melody enveloping your innocuous soul

Nobody on earth could swallow for you other than you yourself, in order to let breath flow like an uninhibited river of happiness, and at the same ensure that the stomach solely sung the hymns of contentment

Nobody on earth could kiss for you other than you yourself, in order to mélange the avalanche of your ignited emotions with another soul, and thereby perpetually evolve with an unconquerably new fragrance of life

Nobody on earth could dance for you other than you yourself, in order to let every incarcerated vindication of your monotonous bones liberate into the surreal pulse of rhythmically palpitating night

Nobody on earth could achieve for you other than you yourself, in order to grant every nerve under your skin the essence of unparalleled contentment and chart your own infallible course to victory amidst a pack of satanic wolves

Nobody on earth could embrace for you other than you yourself, in order to timelessly coalesce every fabric of your existence with the religion of living-kind, and thus feel the most insuperably blessed entity alive

Nobody on earth could procreate for you other than you yourself, in order that you play your own distinctively significant part in continuing God's chapter of creation, in perfect symbiosis with the beats of nature divine

Nobody on earth could hear for you other than you yourself, in order to form your very own unduplicated perception of everything happening around you, undeterred by the tyrannical bigotry of the planet outside

Nobody on earth could die for you other than you yourself, in order that you quit breath solely on the commands of the Omnipresent Almighty Lord, and make way for a fresher new civilization of magical goodness

Nobody on earth could live for you other than you yourself, in order to be an integral element of the drapery of this effervescent planet and further embellish each step that you tread with the spirit of immortal love

Then why do you keep weeping that you are all alone, when you have in fact the most invincibly blessed company on earth to disseminate love, friendship and undying charm—which is, by the Grace of God, none other but you yourself.

Leave me alone

Leave me alone to battle my loneliness till the time I
emerge irrevocably triumphant, sprint forward in
untamed exhilaration to bask in the full fervor of life

Leave me alone to experience each unfurling moment
as it painstakingly unveils, retrospect my cherished
moments of the past, when I innocuously bounced on
the sacrosanct lap of my mother

Leave me alone to uninhibitedly free each of my
despairingly frazzled senses, incessantly fantasize in
the aisles of augmenting desire, yearning for all the
bountifully ravishing beauty on this planet

Leave me alone to do what I was stupendously best in,
pave a blazing path of my own, far away from the
interruptions of the monotonously lackadaisical
society

Leave me alone to explore the more intricate nuances
of life, to frolic with orphaned children through the
mushy meadows, bringing back a smile to their
impoverished lives

Leave me alone to express the most innermost voices
of my conscience, indefatigably meditate to search for
that righteousness that had so miserably eluded me all
my life

Leave me alone to wholeheartedly embrace my fellow
comrades in inexplicable agony, philander with
whomsoever I desired, irrespective of caste, creed and
indiscriminate racial malice

Leave me alone to fanatically pursue the art profusely
embodied in my blood, intransigently drowning
myself into an ocean of unfathomable enthrallment

Leave me alone to wander like a prince under the
milky beams of moonlight, languidly doze dreaming
about paradise in profoundly sweltering sunshine that
illuminates the day

Leave me alone to passionately follow the holistic
ideals of humanity, wholesomely freeing myself from
the tyrannically dictatorial norms of the spurious
world outside

Leave me alone to elope to the astronomical summits
of longing whenever I like, then crawl back lamely on
mundane soil for hours immemorial

Leave me alone to construct my dwelling in the most
exact way I like, stuffing each of its walls with the
spirit of unprecedented brotherhood and harmony,
alike

Leave me alone to vivaciously evolve every
unearthing second, create incredulously magnificent
wonders from the esoterically enigmatic imagery
which turbulently revolves in my mind

Leave me alone to dance with the voluptuously divine
angel of my dreams, eternalize my every blossoming
tomorrow with the poignantly charismatic empathy in
my mate's eyes

Leave me alone to melodiously sing the rhymes of
vibrantly flowering nature, be profoundly mesmerized
by the chirping of the nightingale, the roaring of the
royal lion, alike

Leave me alone to perpetually inscribe in my soul the names that I profusely cherish, ubiquitously disseminate the message of immortal peace and solidarity to every parasite sucking innocent blood outside

Leave me alone to pen down countless lines of philanthropic literature in a single day, incorrigibly blend with the tunes that flow from each of my senses, for infinite more births yet to come

Leave me alone to forever bond with the love of my life, breaking free from the satanically hostile chains of contemporary tradition and bombastic imprisonment

Leave me alone to romance, to dream, to share, to imbibe, more importantly to live life the way I want it to unfold, the way God has made me and beautifully endowed me to be.

Life's the way you see it

For some it was a garden of bountifully mesmerizing
roses, while some could only indefatigably witness the
acrimoniously pugnacious thorns

For some it was a surreally rhapsodic cloud showering
perennial enchantment, while some could only
relentlessly feel penalized by the shades of
gruesomely pulverizing black

For some it was a forest of panoramically evergreen
vivaciousness, while some could only fretfully rebuke
the enigmatically inexplicable travails and trails

For some it was an ocean of unsurpassably
unassailable happiness, while some could only
unrelentingly blame the maliciously lambasting
maelstrom of pernicious waves

For some it was an unflinching fortress of timelessly
blissful solidarity, while some could only implacably
feel the disparagingly deteriorating abrasions with the
inevitably unstoppable unfurling of time

For some it was a tantalizingly celestial nightingale,
while some could only dogmatically curse the
inconspicuous pinches of harmlessly holistic
adulteration in the air

For some it was a meadow of eternally priceless
peace, while some could only incorrigibly experience
the frigid chunks of obnoxiously threadbare dirt

For some it was a fireball of insuperably untamed passion, while some could only intractably feel outlandishly intimidated by the wisps of hideously black smoke, which disastrously obfuscated their vision

For some it was an ebulliently fathomless book of unendingly euphoric adventure, while some could only wearyingly feel asphyxiated by the sheer and inexplicably unfurling volume

For some it was a bountifully persevering ladder to eternal success, while some could only intransigently castigate the unfathomable array of steep stairs

For some it was an unbelievable rainbow of heavenly versatility, while some could only ruthlessly feel the incomprehensibly endless festoon of harsh shades

For some it was an Omnipotent Sun of invincibly righteous hope, while some could only acrimoniously feel the boundlessly austere rays left, right and spurious center

For some it was an iridescently twinkling star of unprecedented optimism, while some could only remorsefully feel the infinitesimally uncanny flicker inflamingly imperil their sanctimonious existence

For some it was an immortally patriotic march towards glorious martyrdom, while some could only grievingly feel the blood-soaked sacrifices in the triumphant odyssey in between

For some it was an unshakably sacrosanct mother who timelessly proliferate God's Omnipresent chapter of survival, while some could only preposterously feel the savage waves of bedlam labour pain, in between

O Yes! For some it was an indomitably victorious
inferno of passionately loving heartbeats, while some
could only limitlessly grouse the reverberating sound,
ignominiously admonishing it for bringing cacophony
in their dwindling stride

Because although the Omniscient Creator had
bestowed it in the most holistically unconquerable of
forms upon every organism symbiotically alike,
Life's the way you choose it to be
Life's the way you make it
Life's the way you believe it to be
Life's the way you see it.

Live and let live

Smile philanthropically, and let others smile too, to
their ultimate heart's content

Fly uninhibitedly, and let others fly like a prince too,
through the majestically bountiful cocoon of crimson
clouds

Wink flirtatiously, and let others wink too, through the
aisles of unprecedented desire and rhapsodically
ardent happiness

Gallop enthusiastically, and let others gallop too, in
untamed frenzy through the mystically alluring hills,
drowned in the golden light of the dazzling fire body
of the Sun

Donate chivalrously, and let others donate too, with all
the goodness assimilated in their magnanimously
benevolent souls

Embrace passionately, and let others embrace too,
with thunderbolts of ardent yearning, escalating
perennially in their impoverished souls

Sing melodiously, and let others sing too, unveiling
the innermost arenas of their enslaved conscience, into
ebulliently captivating sound

Dance tantalizingly, and let others dance too, diffusing
waves of unrelenting passion in the heart of the
romantically philandering midnight

Fantasize intransigently, and let others fantasize too,
basking in the glory of unfathomably stupendous
beauty around, being perpetually entrenched by the
magnificence of this enigmatically alluring Universe

Talk dynamically, and let others talk too, discovering
a new-found confidence in their voice, the sound
lingering in each iota of their blood, to make them feel
the most blissful entities alive

Share generously, and let others share too,
ubiquitously disseminating the essence of everlasting
humanity, to march forward as the strongest
civilization, alike

Evolve intriguingly, and let others evolve too,
innocuously harnessing each ingenious idea of theirs
into the corridors of a celestial paradise

Bond compassionately, and let others bond too, in
threads of invincible harmony and mutual symbiosis,
together defending against the mightiest of
acrimonious attacks on this planet

Walk flamboyantly, and let others walk too,
enchantingly leading each day as it is unleashed,
persevering with stupendous honesty and fortitude
towards their ultimate mission in life

Philander charismatically, and let others philander too,
exploring all the incredulously ravishing beauty on
this earth, blossoming each instant into an
unbelievable festoon of joyous ecstasy

Romanticize exotically, and let others romanticize too,
enlightening their lives, as well as that of their fellow
mates, with optimistic hope and vivaciously vibrant
celebration

Breathe royally, and let others breathe too, exhaling
each puff of air with insurmountable exhilaration to
lead countlessly more magnetically enriching lives

Love immortally, and let others love too, bonding
each heart across the complexion of this gigantic
globe with the impregnable ocean of compassionate
empathy

Live like a King, and let others live too, soaring
higher than the clouds every unveiling minute of
Oligarchic existence, gushing forward like an
euphoric whirlwind as each chapter of joy and pain,
unfurls inexplicably in life.

Life is beautiful

Every minute unleashing all day is a beautiful minute,
getting you acclimatized with the pace of life

Every flower protruding from soil is a beautiful
flower, spreading its mesmerizing scent deeply into
your nostrils

Every face smiling in the universe is a beautiful face,
brilliantly portraying its visage

Every bird flying in the cosmos is a beautiful bird,
overwhelming your ears with its melodious sounds

Every mountain towering towards the sky is a
beautiful mountain, appeasing your eyes with its
picturesque landscapes

Every root of grass projecting from the jungle is a
beautiful root, tingling your senses, making you
exotically dream

Every hand that serves philanthropically is a beautiful
hand, propagating an egalitarian spirit in whomsoever
it caresses

Every stream that flows through land is a beautiful
stream, pacifying the thirst of several scorched in the
vicinity

Every eye that views goodness in this world is a
beautiful eye, sharing empathy with millions of the
bereaved lying around

Every cloud in the sky is a beautiful cloud, showering
droplets of euphoric rain on earth, shielding it from
the acerbic rays of the sun

Every language spoken is a beautiful language, assisting a person to convey his innermost of feelings

Every mirror embedded on the walls is a beautiful mirror, portraying to you your candid reflection

Every color that circumvents your visage is a beautiful color, symbolizing the oneness of the human race

Every voice that emanates from the throat is a beautiful voice, explicitly expressing a person's needs and desires

Every mind impregnated within the skull is a beautiful mind, having the unfathomable ability to achieve the impossible

Every foot which walks innocently is a beautiful foot, leaving behind a trail of holistic footprints

Every leaf that extrudes from the tree is a beautiful leaf, entrenching the dull with shades of everlasting green

Every mother having delivered a child is a beautiful mother, continuing the wonderful process of evolution

Every heart imprisoned inside the chest is a beautiful heart, passionately throbbing when struck by an ensemble of emotions

And every entity trespassing through the surface of this earth is a beautiful entity, making the globe a beautiful place to live, giving rise to the famous and immortal adage, which proudly proclaims that "LIFE IS BEAUTIFUL".

Stop feeling sorry

If you're perennially smiling, don't feel sorry at all for
all those whose innocuous cheeks are inundated with
nothing else but an unsurpassable whirlpool of tears

If you're blazingly intrepid, don't feel sorry at all for
all those who uncontrollably quaver at even the most
inconspicuous whisper of the evanescently cowardly
wind

If you're stupendously white, don't feel sorry at all for
all those whose skins were jinxed with a color more
acrimoniously black than the most pathetically
blackened of charcoal

If you're bountifully virile, don't feel sorry at all for
all those who couldn't proliferate into even a
mercurial shadow of themselves, even in the most
astoundingly pristine of their youth

If you're unbelievably creative, don't feel sorry at all
for all those whose brains were in a state of
amorphously stony inertia right since the very first cry
of euphorically resplendent birth

If you're invincibly strong, don't feel sorry at all for
all those whose frigid veins disdainfully popped out of
their impoverished skins, whose stomachs shriveled
into recesses of nothingness forever and ever and ever

If you're amazingly eclectic, don't feel sorry at all for
all those whose robotic footsteps led them to nowhere
else but the most blasphemously delinquent graves of
nonsensical monotony

If you're incomparably wealthy, don't feel sorry at all
for all those who spent every unfurling instant of their
horrifically dismantled lifetime within the lecherously
incarcerated confines of the parsimonious guttersnipe

If you're spell-bindingly robust, don't feel sorry at all
for all those who are afflicted with the most
invidiously penalizing of cancer/aids, for whom death
is the most inevitably sadistic signature of life

If you're ebulliently athletic, don't feel sorry at all for
all those whose bodies are indescribably maimed,
tawdrily thwarted into disparaging oblivion for
ostensibly no fault of their own

If you're unfathomably sensitive, don't feel sorry at
all for all those whose ears aren't anything but jewels
without the slightest luster, as brutal strokes of destiny
have limitlessly rendered them stone-deaf

If you're miraculously hawk-eyed, don't feel sorry at
all for all those who can sight nothing but a corpse of
crucifying blackness in front of their eyes, even under
the most omnipotently brilliant of sunlight

If you're mellifluously sweet-tongued, don't feel sorry
at all for all those whose tongues blurted nothing but
inanely incomprehensible balderdash, as the thorns of
decrepit dumbness had stung them right in the center
of their spines

If you're beautifully sculptured, don't feel sorry at all
for all those whose faces inadvertently resemble the
most preposterously distorted of dinosaurs

If you're inevitably magnetic, don't feel sorry at all for all those whose countless zillion efforts still miserably flounder to entice the heart of even an ethereally insouciant fly

If you're brilliantly patriotic, don't feel sorry at all for all those who prefer to sell their mothers and their souls, instead of mustering the tenacity to take the onslaught of the rampaging devil on their barren chests

If you're altruistically sacrosanct, don't feel sorry at all for all those who spent almost every unleashed second of their devastated lives on the ultimate precipices of mental retardation and in a dilapidated mental asylum

If you're unassailably breathing, don't feel sorry at all for all those whose life was just for the sake of the externally worthless physical form, whose souls had died the ghastliest of deaths at the hands of torturous fate, infinite births ago

If you're immortally in love, don't feel sorry at all for all those whose beats did quintessentially liberate into the atmosphere like yours, but unfortunately failed to coalesce with the eternally fructifying and ultimate love of their life

Because
The instant you start to feel the least sorry for all these kinds of organisms and countless more hopelessly deprived of their kind, you'd be in fact giving them an instantaneous death which would be more gory than the goriest of deaths could ever be, deaths caused by sympathetic disdain, deaths caused by your attitude of crumbling weakness, deaths caused by your feeling of

sheer helplessness, deaths caused by your inability to
accept them as blessedly normal entities alive

While
the instant you stopped feeling sorry for them,
wholeheartedly embracing them instead, as just one of
your blessed kind, the instant you selflessly reached
out to even the most infinitesimal aspect of theirs, the
instant you tried and did your very best for them,
blending each of your gregarious breaths with theirs,
that very instant, and by the grace of God, you'd not
only be attaining the most supreme epitome of
divinity, but commencing upon an expedition, united
with them, to exist as the most priceless,
unconquerable form of celestial living kind.

Undefeated life

Every despairingly devastating darkness, which you
encountered in your way, eventually proves to be an
irrefutable way, victoriously leading you to the
corridor of optimistically scintillating brilliance

Every horrendously diabolical impediment, which you
encountered in your way, eventually proves to be an
unconquerable ray, blissfully unfurling into the
paradise of everlastingly blossoming prosperity

Every viciously traumatic whirlwind, which you
encountered in your way, eventually proves to be an
invincible messiah, insatiably propelling you on the
path of magnificently tranquil euphoria

Every tyrannically debilitating disease, which you
encountered in your way, eventually proves to be an
impregnable elixir, ebulliently making you enjoy
every instant of rhapsodically redolent life

Every morbidly stony wall, which you encountered in
your way, eventually proves to be a resplendent sky,
vibrantly enshrouding your haplessly shattered senses
with bountiful timelessness

Every sardonically cynical abuse, which you
encountered in your way, eventually proves to be a
unassailable fortress of solidarity, bestowing you with
the tenacity to perennially flower in the chapter of
mystically replenishing existence

Every brutally savage kick, which you encountered in
your way, eventually proves to be an unflinching path
to blazing success, embracing each iota of your
miserably dwindling existence with overwhelmingly
unsurpassable fortitude

Every satanic whirlpool of tears, which you
encountered in your way, eventually proves to be a
waterfall of everlasting jubilation, perpetuating each
of your drearily dolorous nerves with the mantra of
altruistic contentment

Every dungeon of horrifically salacious boredom,
which you encountered in your way, eventually proves
to be a blanket of compassionately enthralling
enthusiasm,
becoming your most invaluably glorious asset to soar
high each instant of life

Every indiscriminately uncouth rejection, which you
encountered in your way, eventually proves to be an
astoundingly panoramic rainbow of triumph, with the
entire Universe saluting your inherently benevolent
prowess

Every coldblooded meal of stone, which you
encountered in your way, eventually proves to be a
ravishingly eternal fruit of Nature's euphoric creation,
divinely pacifying your savagely frazzled demeanor

Every grotesquely ghastly distortion, which you
encountered in your way, eventually proves to be an
island of exhilarating charisma, blessing each of your
barbarically anguished veins with magically
miraculous enchantment

Every ominously malicious hostility, which you
encountered in your way, eventually proves to be a
gloriously marvelous dusk of victory, beamingly
bequeathing upon you the never-dying spirit of
timeless survival

Every painstakingly feeble globule of sweat, which
you encountered in your way, eventually proves to be
the scent of astronomical courage, unequivocally
escalating you into the clouds of bloomingly
unshakable success

Every disdainfully disgusting dirt, which you
encountered in your way, eventually proves to be a
planet of irrevocable purity, beautifully cleansing
every pore of your devastated countenance with the
profuse yearning to forever surge forward in life

Every lecherously abominable hatred, which you
encountered in your way, eventually proves to be a
fountain of pricelessly unconquerable love,
unbelievably caressing each invidiously corrupt
element of your soul with the sparkling goodness of
creation

And every vindictively sullen corpse of death, which
you encountered in your way, eventually proves to be
a divine sky of existence, making you immortally
stand up to the devil and gloriously spawn once again
into a tale of mystically undefeated life.

The walls were my very best friends

The walls were my very best friends as I boisterously
conversed with them for hours immemorial, after the
closest around me had turned a deaf ear to even the
most brilliant of achievements, some shunning me due
to lack of time, some shunning me brutally due to
prejudice

The walls were my very best friends, as I shared the
most eccentric of my secrets with their invincible
hardness. Because if I did the same with society
outside, it would pounce and exploit me to the fullest
for my deficiencies up till the last breath I exhaled

The walls were my very best friends, as I adorned
them with infinite lines of spell-binding poetry, after
the actual girl I'd written them for preposterously
ridiculed them and torched them alive

The walls were my very best friends, as I banged my
fists and legs against them infinite times, after the
pangs of livid isolation and worldly subterfuge had
thwarted me beyond any conceivable realm of sanctity

The walls were my very best friends, as I unabashedly
wept the most intricate woes of my heart against their
impregnable stoicism, after my cherished near and
dear labeled me as only an emotional fool because of
the heartfelt moisture in my eyes

The walls were my very best friends, as I sang
countless tunes of peace towards their united oneness,
after all I was coerced to do by my relatives was work
from 9 to 9 like a robot in the malicious corporate
world outside

The walls were my very best friends, as they
altruistically saw me for what I was originally born as;
and not for money, status, sanctimonious position in
the society that I'd vapidly attained

The walls were my very best friends, as they blissfully
sheltered even the most evanescent of my shadows
and desires, after all that blew outside was
acrimonious wisps of smoke and pugnacious war

The walls were my very best friends, as I
wholesomely leaned upon them whilst eating my
food, sleeping and tingling adventure, after the natural
environment, trees and wildlife were satanically
bombarded by materialistic man outside

The walls were my very best friends, as I
uninhibitedly perpetuated them with my footprints,
thumbprints and veritable signatures, after no other
parchment of paper or space on this parasitic earth,
was ready to accept them

The walls were my very best friends, as I poignantly
deciphered every intricate thread of my past in their
fathomless recesses and darkness, after my own blood
indefatigably advised me to massacre all emotions
and turn murderously practical

The walls were my very best friends, as I embraced
them wholeheartedly like a child embracing its
mother, finding undefeated compassion in their
egalitarian chest, after no-one else in the world dared
touch my body, grievously afflicted with HIV-AIDS

The walls were my very best friends, as my paintbrush treated them as the ultimate canvas of life, inexhaustibly permeating them with poignantly vivacious color, after my own envious kin wanted my fingers to be cut in broad daylight

The walls were my very best friends, as I exercised against them for unceasing minutes of the day and night, toning each dormant muscle of my body to face the ghastliest of traitors, after every ingredient of the world outside had become the blackness of treacherous war

The walls were my very best friends, as I sought unparalleled inspiration looking at their unshakable periphery, even in the fiercest maelstrom and rain, after every organism in this manipulative world today trying to endlessly pin me down

The walls were my very best friends, ardently listening to each of my passionately throbbing heartbeats, after all that the alien globe gave them was an unsurpassable graveyard of licentious betrayal

The walls were my very best friends, unnervingly allowing me to breathe ecstatically down their naked nape, after my own revered beloved discarded me disdainfully like reproachful shit, declaring my breath as foul.

A heart for another heart

An eye for another eye would definitely plunge
the entire world into a mortuary of cringing
darkness—would definitely make the entire world
blind

A tongue for another tongue would definitely dumb
the entire world into a wall of haplessly delirious
silence—would definitely make the entire world mute

An ear for another ear would definitely plague
the entire world into a unfathomably deep gorge of
sadistic nothingness – would definitely make the
entire world deaf

A lip for another lip would definitely devastate the
entire world into a corpse of irrevocably jinxed
sadness— would definitely make the entire world
flagrantly morose

A hand for another hand would definitely plummet the
entire world into a carcass of fetidly indescribable
hopelessness—would definitely make the entire world
beg beyond holistic heights

A spine for another spine would definitely incarcerate
the entire world into chains of sacrilegiously
blackened slavery—would definitely make the entire
world denigrated beyond self respect

A stomach for another stomach would definitely
emaciate the entire world into infinite skulls of
reproachful hunger—would definitely make the entire
world vindictively starve

A neck for another neck would definitely curse the entire world into an inconsolably hideous dungeon of emptiness—would definitely make the entire world a bloodily anarchist battlefield

A vein for another vein would definitely devastate the entire world into demonically sadistic lacunae—would definitely make the entire world plaintively emotionless

A skin for another skin would definitely freeze the entire world into a gutter-pipe of shivering and cloistered hopelessness—would definitely make the entire world crumble even under the strongest of blistering Sun

A shoulder for another shoulder would definitely deteriorate the entire world into a slush-pile of abysmally pitiful remorse—would definitely make the entire world directionless

A leg for another leg would definitely sink the entire world into the marshes of despondently orphaned doomsday—would definitely make the whole world forlornly maimed

A bone for another bone would definitely squelch the entire world beyond the threshold of unimaginable despair—would definitely make the whole world irrevocably maimed

A tooth for another tooth would definitely bruise the entire world into dastardly tastelessness—would definitely make the whole world remorsefully bland

A cheek for another cheek would definitely distort the entire world into a coffin of crucified ugliness—would definitely make the entire world a perennially maudlin scarecrow

A blood-drop for another blood-drop would definitely metamorphose the entire world into a veritably breathing hell—would definitely make the entire world a reproachfully stinking ghost

Whist a HEART for another HEART—-would definitely immortalize the entire world into the religion of eternal mankind—-make the entire world fall forever and ever and ever without a chance to ever rise up into the ocean of immortal humanity and love.

Godly letter "I"

You might say that letter "I" singularly by itself was
disgustingly conceited, and brought along with it only
a dungeon of haplessly asphyxiating doom

You might say that letter "I" singularly by itself was
chauvinistically male, and brought along with it only a
maelstrom of pessimistically demented energy

You might say that letter "I" singularly by itself was
devastatingly deteriorating, and brought along with it
only a gutter of ignominiously fetid malevolence

You might say that letter "I" singularly by itself was
atrociously invidious, and brought along with it only a
mortuary of indiscriminately ghastly meaninglessness

You might say that letter "I" singularly by itself was
vindictively obstreperous, and brought along with it
only a coffin of despairingly treacherous defeat

You might say that letter "I" singularly by itself was
drearily egocentric, and brought along with it
only a nightfall of never endingly maiming blackness

You might say that letter "I" singularly by itself was
intolerably blasphemous, and brought along with it
only a fecklessly oblivious vacuum of ungainly
remorsefulness

You might say that letter "I" singularly by itself was
robotically insane, and brought along with it only a
holocaust of indelibly ribald obsessiveness

You might say that letter "I" singularly by itself was
demonically perverted, and brought along with it
only a jailhouse of treacherously massacring madness

You might say that letter "I" singularly by itself was
tyrannically lambasting, and brought along with it
only a carcass of ominously demeaning expletives

You might say that letter "I" singularly by itself was
cadaverously fulsome, and brought along with it
only tears of inexplicably assassinating gloom

You might say that letter "I" singularly by itself was
lethally crucifying, and brought along with it
only a graveyard of doggedly unbearable stench

You might say that letter "I" singularly by itself was
hedonistically slandering, and brought along with it
only a preposterously gory shadow of disdain

You might say that letter "I" singularly by itself
was agonizingly incarcerating, and brought along with
it only a dust storm of profanely decrepit
rebelliousness

You might say that letter "I" singularly by itself was
pugnaciously disconcerting; and brought along with it
only a haplessly excoriating bed of venomous thorns

You might say that letter "I" singularly by itself; was
preposterously ludicrous; and brought along with it;
only falsely sycophantic winds of wretched
wantonness

You might say that letter "I" singularly by itself was
devilishly beheading, and brought along with it only
the footsteps of licentiously whipping hell

You might say that letter "I" singularly by itself was
inconspicuously imbecile, and brought along with it
only the cancerous blisters of hopelessly disparaging
extinction

You might say that letter "I" singularly by itself was unacceptably dictatorial; and brought along with it only the ghosts of sinfully plundering selfishness

But have you ever wondered that unless and until you endlessly love your own self, unless and until you commence to timelessly admire every facet of your divinely blessed existence, unless and until you unflinchingly worship the "I" in your very own self, How can you ever dream of loving and wholesomely embracing others?
How can you ever dream of reaching out to and immortally bonding with every echelon of bountiful living kind?

Because for you to dream of, or ever dare of becoming the united "We", you inevitably need to start first with your very own self; you inevitably need to start with the godly letter "I".

The greatest victory

The greatest victory for a mother was, when she was
able invincibly to protect her child from all evil
lurking rampantly in the night and marathon hours of
the sunlit day

The greatest victory for a soldier was, when he
valiantly bore the hostile opposition, waved the flag of
his country in the heart of the colossal enemy camp

The greatest victory for a spotted panther was, when it
mercilessly capsized its prey by the neck, ripped it
apart into boundless fragments before handsomely
devouring it down

The greatest victory for the black conglomerate of
clouds was, when despite the fulminating fire-ball of
Sun behind, they were able to pour down
indefatigably upon the surface of the earth

The greatest victory for the inconspicuous little
mosquito was, when it sucked gallons of blood from
robust flesh, dexterously evaded all in the vicinity
who tried to capture it

The greatest victory for the mammoth shark was,
when it unsparingly toppled over the mighty ship with
her snout, gobbled each of its passengers to satisfy its
gluttony for the unveiling hour

The greatest victory for the diminutive red ant was,
when she stung the gigantic elephant on his feet, made
him plummet to the ground and taste dust like a pack
of molten matchsticks

The greatest victory for the ocean was, that it never dried irrespective of the most acerbic of droughts, kept swirling with its ravishing waves striking astoundingly against the rocks

The greatest victory for the gleaming axe was, when it sliced gargantuan stalks of the century-old tree with sheer disdain, engendering the lanky stem to collapse with a sigh on the mud

The greatest victory for the lips was, when they were able to passionately kiss the girl they desired, taking complete control over her mind, body, and soul

The greatest victory for the tabby cat was, when she sprang upon clusters of unsuspecting mice, masticated them with whole-hearted relish as the first rays of dawn crept from the sky

The greatest victory for the blazing fire was, when it charred to raw soot whatever dared trespass into its blistering path

The greatest victory for the devotee was, when he was able to appease the creator with his overwhelming devotion and penance, rise to the pinnacle of success with the blessings of Almighty God

The greatest victory for the eye was, when it was able to sight the most mesmerizing places in this Universe, keep staring for times immemorial deeply into the eyes of the person it revered and loved

The greatest victory for the hideously wailing vulture was, when it viciously plucked out flesh from the body of the dead, feasted on its meal with a flame of exultation burning in its eyes

The greatest victory for the infinite territories of the sprawling desert was, when it was able to entice millions of unsuspecting adventurers, luring them with its fake mirages which were nothing else but pure sand

The greatest victory for the blood flowing in the body was, when it blended with the soil in which it was born

And the greatest victory for Man on this planet was, when he knew himself thoroughly, conquered all his desires and emotions, joined hands with his fellow comrades, putting in his ultimate in order to save humanity.

The other aim of life

The other aim of life is to spawn into a rhapsodically
fresh beginning every unfurling minute of the day,
although your past might have indiscriminately
pulverized you with infinite whiplashes of abuse and
hedonistic disdain

The other aim of life is to unfurl into an unsurpassable
festoon of resplendently vivacious color, be enamored
by the fathomlessly panoramic gorges of Almighty
Lord, even while you were in drearily subjugated
sleep

The other aim of life is to frolic in the aisles of
rapaciously uncontrollable desire, kiss the most
unprecedented apogees of success, even when you felt
you were being ruthlessly gored by the ferociously
decimating bull

The other aim of life is to unflinchingly confront the
most venomous juggernaut of the evil, perennially
smiling with the blessings of the Omnipotent divine

The other aim of life is to metamorphose even the
most ethereal trace of deliriously pernicious insanity,
into an unrelenting tornado of exuberantly
mesmerizing freshness

The other aim of life is to uninhibitedly philander
under the perpetually blazing rays of the Omniscient
Sun, enlightening every dwelling besieged with
cancerously arcane despair, even though you were
standing beside your veritable shivering grave

The other aim of life is to symbiotically prosper, arm in arm, with every echelon of living kind and holistic society, mélangeing every conceivable color under the Sun with the religion of unconquerable humanity

The other aim of life is to keep perennially blossoming into a civilization of fructifying virility, boundless kilometers away from the tombstones of morbidly decrepit manipulation and baselessly lugubrious prejudice

The other aim of life is to assimilate all goodness that you could fathom from the enchantingly spell-binding atmosphere, ubiquitously sprinkle and bestow the same upon every entity that you encountered in your enigmatic way

The other aim of life is to keep relentlessly blazing like into a whirlpool of artistically untamed exoticism, even as avalanches of grumpily sodomizing politics tried to slander and lethally incarcerate you from all sides

The other aim of life is to regally lead each unfurling moment that unleashed your way to the most aristocratic limits, and limitlessly ensure the same to every bereaved organism, frantically struggling to be alive

The other aim of life is to tirelessly spawn like the poignantly seductive dewdrop, even though it was well past the heart of gruesomely tyrannizing midnight

The other aim of life is to indomitably stand for the unassailably righteous redolence of Omnipresent truth, topple over the monsters of hell with the sword of timelessly sacrosanct unity

The other aim of life is to indefatigably march on the mission to bond all estranged and disparagingly staggering mankind with threads of unbreakably euphoric and propitiously beautiful camaraderie

The other aim of life is to soar like a handsomely unblemished prince through the heavens of bountiful oneness, blissfully perpetuate the mantra of iridescent sharing amongst all cold-bloodedly dreadful parasites

The other aim of life is to unstoppably innovate a civilization of peerless jubilation all the time, trigger the element of congenital restlessness in your soul to harness the most enthrallingly optimum of even the most frigid bits of lackadaisical space

The other aim of life is to be a messiah of all opprobriously decaying living kind, dissipating the unfathomably majestic energy of your persona to give birth to an immortally optimistic tomorrow

The other aim of life is to take birth infinite times again and again and again for the beloved whom you had wholesomely dedicated your present life to

And the other aim of life is always to follow the innermost voices of your heart, coalesce even the most diminutive ingredient of your blood with the spirit of divinely compassionate sensuality, even as the entire uncouthly monotonous world outside treated you as the devil's wife.

The true spirit of life

In order to bring out the true essence of a rose, you
need to place it in the strong currents of a misty breeze

In order to bring out the true sparkle of a diamond,
you need to scrub it vigorously with a coarse chunk of
cloth

In order to bring out the true flavor of milk, you need
to tenaciously extract the same from the sacrosanct
demeanor of mother cow

In order to bring out the true softness of scalp hair,
you need to meticulously entangle the disdainful
clusters, swish the hair brush animatedly all over

In order to bring out the true aroma of swirling waves,
you need to make them collide with the mammoth
conglomerate of shining rocks

In order to bring out the true color of the sky, you
need to inundate it with dazzling beams of sunlight

In order to bring out the true taste of succulent apple,
you need to masticate the same with overwhelming
ardor

In order to bring out the true strength of cement, you
need to sprinkle it with small pints of water every day,
granting it fortification with every hour unleashing

In order to bring out the true heat of sand, you need to
let it sizzle in the hostile light rays of the afternoon
sun

In order to bring out the true complexion of the
chameleon, you need to let it philander freely in
constantly changing surroundings

In order to bring out the true size of the preposterously
huge whale, you need to place it in a pond replete with
small fish

In order to bring out the true transparency of a mirror,
you need to sight your reflection in the same at an
hour past unearthly midnight

In order to bring out the true scent of nondescript
mud, you need flood the same with infinite globules
of the fresh water of rain

In order to bring out the true voice of the nightingale,
you need to provide it with a perpetually still
ambience to sing its melodious tunes

In order to bring out the true smile of a child, you
need to hoist it high in the air, kiss and tickle it
voraciously in its ribs

In order to bring out the true speed of the panther, you
need to entice him with a flock of nimble-footed deer
galloping through the forest

In order to bring out the true belligerence of a soldier,
you need to place him against his adversary on the
merciless battlefield

In order to bring out the true fervor of love, you need
to stand by your beloved till time immemorial

And in order to bring out the "TRUE SPIRIT OF LIFE", you need to plunge into the sea of vivacious adventure, confront a plethora of acerbic barricades, and yet come out of it all guns blazing.

Man: the maker of his own destiny

It was perhaps natural if the deserts blamed the
flaming Sun for acrimoniously blistering into
tumultuous heat, as they were perpetually unable to do
anything other than just relentlessly whirl into a pool
of disdainful dust and mirage all night and brilliant
day

It was perhaps natural if the trees blamed the vengeful
hurricanes for devastating their blissful entity into an
inconspicuously bedraggled heap, as they were
perpetually unable to anything other than just
incessantly embed their roots deeper and deeper into
stony cocoons of lackluster soil

It was perhaps natural if the crops blamed the
torrential floods for wholesomely disorienting them
into pools of frigidly soiled banana skins, as they were
perpetually unable to do anything other than just
obediently sway in the direction of the nimble
winds

It was perhaps natural if the frogs blamed the
despondent well for perniciously incarcerating them
into dungeons of despair, as they were perpetually
unable to do anything other than just loquaciously
leaping within the interiors for countless more
births yet to unveil

It was perhaps natural if the oceans blamed the fleet of
ominously advancing ships for profusely adulterating
their ravishingly tantalizing waters, as they were
perpetually unable to do anything other than just
tirelessly undulate into a fountain of rhapsodically
tangy froth

It was perhaps natural if the grass blamed the
treacherously trampling juggernaut of trucks for
squashing them indiscriminately into graveyards of
horrendous death, as they were perpetually unable to
do anything other than just fluttering in unbelievably
aristocratic unison to the commands of the seductively
enthralling breeze

It was perhaps natural if the mountains blamed the
brutally freezing snow for making them ludicrously
shiver even in the heart of the flamboyantly boisterous
day, as they were perpetually unable to do anything
other than just gigantically tower into the
handsome gorge of clouds for boundless more births
yet to unveil

It was perhaps natural if the dungeons blamed the
ominous blackness for barbarically asphyxiating them
in galleries of unsurpassable doom, as they were
perpetually unable to do anything other than just being
timelessly submerge infinite kilometers
beneath the surface of jubilant earth

It was perhaps natural if the nightingale blamed the
ferocious lion for satanically massacring the celestial
melody in its fascinating sound, as it was perpetually
unable to do anything other than just beautifully
unveil the mesmerizing chords of its throat
to incomprehensible ecstasy

It was perhaps natural if the photograph blamed
euphoric vivaciousness for continuously teasing it
beyond the threshold limits of endurance, as it was
perpetually unable to do anything other than just stare
in patient innocuousness infinite hours on the trot

It was perhaps natural if the spider blamed the wildly
whirling winds for decimating its web into a
pulverized junkyard, as it was perpetually unable to do
anything other than just frantically run and suspend
itself nervously from the silken strands

It was perhaps natural if the rainbows blamed the
viciously clandestine clouds for snobbishly
obfuscating their vibrantly resplendent sparkle, as they
were perpetually unable to do anything other than just
vividly sprout up and stringently adhere to
the sky in times of both Sunshine and bountiful rain

It was perhaps natural if the parrots blamed cages for
surreptitiously imprisoning their compassionately
uninhibited freedom, as they were perpetually unable
to do anything other than just cheekily chirp in
innocently holistic tandem

It was perhaps natural if the ants blamed the savagely
marching elephants for squelching them to countless
kilometers beneath their veritably stinking graves, as
they were perpetually unable to do anything other than
just harmlessly squirm in collective troops and
symbiotically upon cold soil

It was perhaps natural if the fruits blamed the
capricious branches of the tree for hurling them
uncouthly towards the apathetic ground at the slightest
draught of breeze, as they were perpetually unable to
do anything other than just robustly augmenting in
shape and size as time merrily elapsed by

But it was unfathomably preposterous if MAN blamed the Almighty Creator for his unrelenting string of ridiculous failures, for although the Omnipotent Lord had majestically spawned him with passionately crimson blood and bone, he was himself and irrefutably the maker of his own destiny.

My faith in God—when I feel I am dying

With every majestic sunset making way for the
Immaculate moon which astoundingly depicts the
multifarious shades of this Universe—which is a gift
from the Omnipotent Creator

With every draught of exuberant wind, which evolves
into a whole new mist of rhapsodic excitement out of
sheer and insipid nothingness

With every dainty petal of the poignant rose, which
permeates a scent of oneness in the otherwise
monotonously subjugated atmosphere

With every vivacious stroke of the mesmerizing
rainbow, which charms the entire Universe, fraught
with its own inexplicably unsolicited misery

With every infinitesimal speck of the atmosphere,
which invincibly cling to the bodies of us living
beings, befriending an entire Universe of solidarity—
from its own realms of isolation and despair

With every step which marches forward to maintain
the royal equilibrium of life, to ensure that life goes on
despite anything and everything, but only by the grace
of God

With every flight of unbridled fantasy, which makes
even the most inconspicuously ordinary of living
beings catapult beyond the definitions of desire

With every squeak which escapes the throat,
triumphantly piercing the bizarre sullenness and
silence of the atmosphere with a desire to be embraced
by one and all

With every sensuously tantalizing night, which unfurls
into the morning of a bountifully optimistic and
brilliant dawn

With every solemn pledge of goodwill in the
graveyard, which bedazzles the ghastly silence of
remorseful death with a new-found longing to
disseminate love and life

With every rumble of inscrutable thunder in the sky,
which brings along with it the optimistic promise of
rain, an infallible reason to cheer in the aisles of
ecstasy

With every inimitably righteous footprint left on soil,
which carves an entire pathway of unflinching
goodness, love and peace, as the quintessential
elements to lead life with

With every idea which uninhibitedly germinates from
the brain, blossoming into boundless sparks of
freshness to unite the entire planet into the religion of
love

With every affable outgrowth which joyously leaps
out of the soil, instantaneously engulfed with the
blessed rays of the Sun after an equally compassionate
cuddling by mother soil

With every handshake executed between people of all
races, religions and colors paving way for the most
immortal and unassailable religion of humanity

With every lump of frigidly asphyxiating snow, which
perseveringly labors its way to becoming the most
adorable stream of love as its eventual outcome

With every step traversing the road not taken,
permeating robotic chunks of the atmosphere with
tantalizing splashes of adventure

With every anecdote of failure which strengthened my
resolve to succeed all the more, metamorphosing
every bit of morbid ash into an opportunity to
holistically survive

My faith in God grew, as irrespective of whatever has
happened or would happen from now on, I know it
would be for the good—As God is my faith, God is
my life—God gives me the power symbiotically to
survive with one and all till the time he commands—
And whenever he decides to take me away from this
earth of his, I sincerely pray to him from my heart and
soul to be able to utter his name in poetry and song
when I feel I am dying.

A gift called life

In order to augment the glory of the crystalline sky,
God inundated it with a festoon of enchantingly misty
clouds

In order to augment the glory of the lanky tree, God
flooded its barren surface with a blanket of fresh green
leaves

In order to augment the glory of the fleshy palm, God
embellished its surface with a myriad of fascinating
lines bifurcated into islands and forks

In order to augment the glory of the plain atmosphere,
God deluged its gloomy ambience with sizzling rays
of brilliant sunlight

In order to augment the glory of the colossal ocean,
God imparted its boundless surface with a cavalcade
of ravishingly frosty waves

In order to augment the glory of fecund territories of
brown soil, God embodied its surface with a wide
fraternity of salubrious crop

In order to augment the glory of the voluptuously
fathomless jungles, God placed a battalion of majestic
lions on its rustled paths

In order to augment the glory of the towering
mountains, God embedded their treacherous slopes
with compassionate balls of white snow

In order to augment the glory of the redolently scarlet
rose, God granted its demeanor with a seductively
exotic scent

In order to augment the glory of the delectably hidden nest, God filled its empty persona with a cluster of stupendously charming and innocuous eggs

In order to augment the glory of the placid night, God blessed its shivering persona with amicably twinkling stars

In order to augment the glory of the gorgeously unsurpassable valley, God lit up its dolorous space with a boisterously pepped up and a stringent echo

In order to augment the glory of the innocuously wandering cow, God imparted it with the prowess of oozing life-yielding and sacrosanct milk

In order to augment the glory of cascading rain, God impregnated the cosmos with a spell-binding and vivacious rainbow

In order to augment the glory of mammoth stacks of diamonds and gold, God triggered their periphery with a mesmerizing and perennial shine

In order to augment the glory of the blind bat, God granted it with the astounding ability to stick wherever it wanted to sleep upside down

In order to augment the glory of the blossoming shoots of bountiful grass, God overwhelmed its tips with tantalizingly alluring dewdrops

In order to augment the glory of true love, God gave it the highest priority on his agendas of this unfathomable Universe, granted it the virtue of being supremely immortal

And in order to augment the glory of every human,
God swamped his dead body with an armory of
passionate heart-beats, flooded his dormant lungs with
gargantuan
bellows of fresh breath, bestowing upon him the most
wonderful gift existing on this planet, a gift which we
all know today as life.

A humble prayer: bless me!

Bless me with the strength to plough through
undulating stretches of fecund land

Bless me with the agility to clamber up serrated skin
of tall pine trees

Bless me with the profound courage to encounter
nefarious criminals head on

Bless me with the ability to discriminate between the
sacrosanct and horrendously bad

Bless me with the nostalgia to reminiscence about
blissful anecdotes of the past and unveiling future

Bless me with the prowess of eloquent speech, for
communication with society

Bless me with the capacity of rescuing urchins
trembling in the arms of fast-approaching death

Bless me with belligerent qualities to become a true
warrior for my revered nation

Bless me with keen eyesight to help a plethora of
citizens traversing the road with strips of black on
their eyes

Bless me with extravagant bulges of body muscle to
stand as a rock between the victimized and lecherous

Bless me with the stupendous power to stay awake at
night enabling me to cover all those shivering with a
woolen quilt

Bless me with bountiful opulence, instigating me to
feed famished masses with twin meals of rice

Bless me with a celestial smile, pacifying hordes of
people in times of disastrous
calamity

Bless me with a chivalrous disposition, making it
easier for me to part with my possessions

Bless me with a down-to-earth attitude, rendering me
versatile to empathize with a myriad of penurious
masses

Bless me with the power to walk barefoot in the
blistering heat, donating my leather boots to those
struck with leprosy

Bless me with an intricate mind deciphering enigmas,
chalking out philanthropic policies for traumatized
prisoners

Bless me with the dexterity to commence my day with
a plain glass of water, relinquishing appetizing meals
served on silver

Bless me with truck-loads of unprejudiced love,
imparting it to all those who indispensably need it

Bless me with the energy to innovate and create,
showering a battalion of contemporary comfort on my
impoverished counterparts

Bless me with the art of holding back my effusive
tears, instead offering tumultuous comfort to the
bereaved

Over and above all O! LORD bless me with the power
to sustain life, succeeding in my endeavor to make
planet earth a better place to live.

A whole new chapter

Every day as you arose at the crackle of mesmerizing
dawn, you blossomed into celestial freshness,
wholesomely shirking the hideously monstrous
monotony of the previous bedraggled day

Every day as you arose at the crackle of blissful dawn,
you wholeheartedly smiled the smile of your life, as
the Omnipotently golden rays of the Sun smooched
you in euphoric entirety

Every day as you arose at the crackle of enchanting
dawn, you became oblivious to the treacherously
barbarous tyrannies meted upon you, as even the most
infinitesimally inane of your senses completely
coalesced with the panoramic mists of mother nature

Every day as you arose at the crackle of rhapsodic
dawn, you devoutly resolved never to repeat your
mistakes of the past, astoundingly trained your every
delinquent nerve to perennially surge forward to
eternal success

Every day as you arose at the crackle of bountiful
dawn, you profoundly reminisced over new memories
of your majestically uninhibited childhood, when you
did not care a damn about this manipulative planet,
compassionately suckling in the lap of your heavenly
mother

Every day as you arose at the crackle of victorious
dawn, you chalked out countless distinct strategies to
irrefutably vanquish the indiscriminately rampaging
devil, inexhaustibly striving for complete freedom of
your mind, body and soul

Every day as you arose at the crackle of poignant dawn, you found the intensity of scarlet blood in your veins more profuse than ever, to holistically survive in times that were good as well as diabolically bad

Every day as you arose at the crackle of Omniscient dawn, you felt an inexorable fervor to discover encapsulating every cranny of your persona, alleviating you from the most severest of your wanton depression, into the aisles of timeless proliferation

Every day as you arose at the crackle of emollient dawn;, you uninhibitedly danced with passionately enthralling ardor, letting every egregiously trapped staleness of your countenance freely cascade out as beautifully fragrant sweat

Every day as you arose at the crackle of philanthropic dawn, you found a boundless array of never-before flavors titillate the buds of your disparagingly emaciated tongue

Every day as you arose at the crackle of immaculate dawn, you tirelessly danced the whites and blacks of your emphatically crystalline eyes to the magically unfurling beams of the pristinely whistling atmosphere

Every day as you arose at the crackle of regale dawn, you flirted with an unfathomable ocean of supreme sensuality, playing hide-n-seek with the evanescently crimson beams of the new-born Sun

Every day as you arose at the crackle of mystical dawn, you unraveled the mortifying introvert in you to the most unprecedented of your capacity, peerlessly blazing in the untamed ardor of intrepidly unflinching life

Every day as you arose at the crackle of jingling dawn, you trod your nimble foot more solidly on earth, more and more invincibly embedding your inimitable rudiments on the landscape of the fathomless globe

Every day as you arose at the crackle of vivacious dawn, you abdicated all your baseless nervousness, scintillated like a true warrior to defend your maliciously usurped and pricelessly venerated motherland

Every day as you arose at the crackle of titillating dawn, you felt every pore of your fecklessly limpid skin, intransigently desirous of being mischievously tickled by the winds of miraculously never-ending procreation

Every day as you arose at the crackle of ecstatic dawn, you felt closer and closer to your impressions on sacred soil, unrelentingly fantasizing about that moment in which was born your very first ancestor

Every day as you arose at the crackle of vivid dawn, you obeisantly surrendered even the most diminutive of your breaths to the unconquerable illumination of the Sun, letting it weave a whole new chapter of your enrapturing existence

And still some of you had the audacity once to say that each new day was fretfully boring, each new day had nothing to offer which was revolutionarily new, each new day brought you closer to your death, each day was just like and nothing but a pathetic facsimile of the very previous day!

An absolute winner

As long as the tree had clusters of leaves covering its
naked body, it was in state of perennial bliss, relaxing
splendidly in the shade, well sequestered from the
acerbic sunshine

As long as the watery eyeball had a fold of brown skin
covering its body, it slept and awoke without the
slightest of effort, as and when it leisurely wanted

As long as the bird had an ensemble of ruffled
feathers covering her body, she displayed
astronomical audacity in soaring high against the most
freezing of winds

As long as the bricks had a fortified coat of cement
covering their body, they felt like the strongest entities
existing on this earth, having the tenacity to resist
even the most tumultuous of earthquake

As long as the raw bones had a blanket of skin
covering their body, they grew and took nourishment
at will, relished the comfort of always being in placid
coolness; while their covering absorbed all of the
sweltering heat

As long as the sky had a cocoon of clouds covering its
body, it was in stupendous rhapsody, being able to
rampantly fantasize at will without the world staring
unrelentingly into its eyes

As long as the conglomerate of yolk and rich protein
had a shell of obdurate white covering its body, it
harnessed and sprouted perfectly, eventually evolving
into a handsome and delectable fledgling with the
passage of time

As long as the flower had a consortium of redolent petals covering its body, it swayed flirtatiously with each draught of wind, twinkled merrily under the star-studded midnight

As long as the teeth had a sheen of enamel to cover their bodies, they uninhibitedly became ready to chew virtually anything, ranging from unripe plums to the hardest of steel circulating in the markets

As long as the candle had an enclosure of emerald glass to cover its body, it burnt flamboyantly with passionate intensity, even in the midst of a cyclonic storm

As long as the golden ink had the capsule of fountain pen to cover its body, it oozed out harmoniously in sporadic intervals, inundating blank sheets of paper with exquisite lines of calligraphy

As long as white electricity had boundless tunnels of plastic to cover its body, it ran at lightening speeds without any fear of hurting anyone, and yet at the same time illuminating the entire township with brilliant light

As long as the child had its mother to cover its tiny body, it bounced boisterously, mischievously smiling and discovering a host of new things every second

As long as the heart had love to cover its throbbing body, it simply refused to quit beating, continued to live and exist immortally beyond the definition of time

And as long as a human being had God to cover his
body, he faced no difficulty whatsoever in leading life,
and in spite of being encapsulated with hordes of
barricades and dilemmas, he always emerged an
absolute winner under the sacrosanct cover of the
Almighty creator.

As long as I had priceless hope

I might be currently in hapless shreds, without even
the most diminutive coin of currency in my
inconspicuously bedraggled pockets,
But as long as I had the jewel of priceless hope in my
soul, I reserved the insurmountable tenacity to
metamorphose every iota of pain into a paradise of
unfettered happiness, as my inevitably destined
moment wholeheartedly descended from the lap of the
Omnipotent Lord Almighty

I might be currently begging discordantly on the stony
streets, without even a strand of infinitesimal saliva to
mellifluously tingle my bereaved throat,
But as long as I had the Sun of optimistic hope in my
soul, I reserved the indomitable power to over-topple
even the mightiest of cannibalistic parasites, as my
inevitably destined moment wholeheartedly
descended from the lap of the bountiful Lord
Almighty

I might be currently feeding myself on pulverized
garbage from the dustbin cover; without a feather of
integrity of my own, as the world relentlessly
lambasted my timidly trembling skin,
But as long as I had the star of resplendent hope in my
soul, I reserved the Herculean prowess of soaring to
the ultimate pinnacles of blazing success, as my
inevitably destined moment wholeheartedly
descended from the lap of the inimitable Lord
Almighty

I might be currently exhaling each breath of mine in
the traumatically beleaguered gutter pipe, without
even the most mercurial strength left in my miserably
bloodstained lips to wholeheartedly smile,
But as long as I had the flower of fragrant hope in my
soul, I reserved the invincible dexterity to spawn into
a sky of unfathomably exhilarating newness, as my
inevitably destined moment wholeheartedly
descended from the lap of the Omnipresent Lord
Almighty

I might be currently staring meaninglessly into
orphaned patches of azure sky, without a single roof
over my head to sequester me from acrimoniously
truculent storm and rain,
But as long as I had the sea of tangy hope in my soul,
I reserved the uncanny mysticism to timelessly charm
even the most lugubriously livid particle of the
atmosphere, as my inevitably destined moment
wholeheartedly descended from the lap of the
unassailable Lord Almighty

I might be currently yawning in supremely fretful
nonchalance, without the slightest of cynosure and
glitterati and with the most venomously lethal
mosquitoes hovering around my hopelessly deserted
skin,
But as long as I had the garland of ingratiating hope in
my soul, I reserved the profound exuberance to
convert even the most bizarrely impossible into the
sky of impregnable success, as my inevitably destined
moment wholeheartedly descended from the lap of the
Omniscient Lord Almighty

I might be currently emaciating with a zillion thorns
of brutal dishonesty being treacherously plundered
into my intestines and without the minutest trace of
dawn in my every unforgivingly imprisoning night,
But as long as I had the rainbow of pristine hope in
my soul, I reserved the untamed ebullience to bare-
footedly adventure into the most fathomless crannies
of this enchanting Universe, as my inevitably destined
moment wholeheartedly descended from the lap of the
ever-pervading Lord Almighty

I might be currently unemployed at all quarters,
without the empathy of a single organism on this
boundlessly enamoring Universe,
But as long as I had the spirit of sacred hope in my
soul, I reserved the infallible energy to blaze into
infinite philanthropically enlightening tomorrows, as
my inevitably destined moment wholeheartedly
descended from the lap of the miraculous Lord
Almighty

And I might be currently devastated and torturously
ripped apart in every aspect of my life, without any
ingredient of this Universe getting stirred by the
unstoppable beating of my impoverished heart,
But as long as I had the fortress of perpetual hope in
my soul, I reserved the uninhibited magnetism to fall
into the oceans of immortally gratifying love, as my
inevitably destined moment wholeheartedly
descended from the lap of unchallengeable Lord
Almighty.

The king of the current moment

The treacherously obsolete yesterday I had
wholesomely forgotten, with even the most
infinitesimal of its vapid impression dissolving into
aisles of frigid nothingness

What was going to happen today I had not the tiniest
of innuendo about, groping into the mercilessly
coldblooded darkness when I pondered upon the same

Tomorrow was a tantalizing mirage, which kept
eluding my invincible grasp
more and more, as I tried indefatigably to snatch it

But nevertheless I was still the unparalleled king of
the current moment, rejoicing in its untamed glory to
the most unprecedented limits, letting its bountiful
majesty take complete control of every one of my
beleaguered veins

The disastrously delirious yesterday had wholesomely
evaporated from my life, with not even the most
vehemently indignant of its maelstroms daring to
come near me

What was going to happen today I had not the most
ephemeral insinuation about, shattering into boundless
fragments of meaninglessness when I tried to
tirelessly envisage the same

Tomorrow was a fathomlessly distant dream, about
whose veritable reality I couldn't figure out head or
spuriously withering tail

But nevertheless I was still the unassailable king of the current moment, letting its unsurpassable enchantment celestially descend upon even the most diminutive cranny of my mind, body and quavering soul

The truculently chauvinistic yesterday had completely deserted the chapter of my life, with not even the most evanescent of its jinxed beam reminiscent in the whites of my eyes

What was going to happen today I had not the most capricious idea about, being banged like a haplessly disoriented coconut against the walls of diabolical hell, when I tried to flex my brain a trifle too much about it

Tomorrow seemed to stretch beyond the realms of my molecular imagination, with the fangs of viciously bellicose uncertainty perpetuating me from all sides

But nevertheless I was still the uninhibited king of the current moment, letting its pragmatically panoramic beauty entirely become the royally seductive veil of my horrendously tyrannized existence

The baselessly crucifying yesterday had entirely abdicated my nimble presence, extinguishing into worthless horizons of irretrievably reproachful oblivion

What was going to happen today I had not the most mercurial of gut feelings
about, being ruthlessly buried alive in coffins of intractable desperation
as I tried valiantly to decipher its ingredients of good and forlornly bad

Tomorrow had still marathon hours to take irrefutably
unshakable
control, with a zillion murderous barricades yet to
overcome

But nevertheless I was still the limitless king of the
current moment,
letting its magnetically divine energy instill
optimistically benign energy
in my delinquent bones to lead countless more
symbiotic lives

The morbidly penalizing yesterday seemed gone since
times immemorial, with
the first rays of Omnipotently brilliant dawn
transcending even the
most non-existent speck of the egregiously rampaging
devil

What was going to happen today I had not the most
ethereal understanding
about, being dissolved into mortuaries of hopeless
insanity when I tried
unambiguously to picture the next hour from now

Tomorrow seemed like it would never come, with the
deplorable conundrum
of murderous manipulation and politics around me,
engendering me to
frenetically search for my every breath

But nevertheless I was still the inimitable king of the
current moment, letting its philanthropically
synergistic heavenliness beautifully coalesce each of
my senses with the mantra of wonderfully egalitarian
mankind, with the spirit of the Ever-Pervading; Divine

Seeking solace

When I felt that the pace of life was overwhelmingly hectic, I sought solace in the blissful backdrop of the mystical valley

When I felt that my legs were indefatigably tired, I sought solace in the king poster bed, tucking them cozily under the frilled mattress

When I felt that each bone impregnated in my body hurt like a thousand corpses, I sought solace in the rejuvenating pool of herbal liquid

When I felt that my tongue had lost all sensation of taste and aroma, I sought solace in a bunch of stupendously seductive grapes dangling in the dense forests

When I felt that my scalp was being attacked by infinite battalions of red ant and termites, I sought solace under the waterfall of medicated shampoo to wholesomely annihilate the last scrap of dirt from its very roots

When I felt that my fingers simply refrained to write, I sought solace in clouds of soft and impeccable cotton, gently caressing each strand and thereby giving maximum ecstasy to my starved flesh

When I felt that my brain had lost all its ability to perceive, monotonously trapped in the disparaging issues of the commercial world, I sought solace in a stream of red wine, gulping down the ravishing elixir to stimulate my dead cells enjoying immortal sleep

When I felt that my feet had gone horrendously numb,
transforming into mammoth slabs of frozen ice, I
sought solace in front of the crackling fire, imparting
to my soles the revitalization to leap in animated
exultation and gallop

When I felt that I was getting insanely bored, with
pangs of uncanny frustration creeping up slowly into
my soul, I sought solace on the boisterous floor of the
vivacious disco, swinging my body to a billion beats
of pulsating music

When I felt that the sweltering rays of the Sun were
piercing with pungent hostility into my skin, I sought
solace in the dainty interiors of my timid and little hut

When I felt that the storm of hunger was brewing up
incorrigibly in my stomach, I sought solace in
shimmering plates inundated with appetizing morsels
of pure curd and steaming rice

When I felt that the stillness of atmosphere was
severely taking its toll on my senses, I sought solace
with the melodiously whistling bird

When I felt that my heart beat was on the verge of
extinction, the throbbing which was once prolifically
violent in my chest now not heard at all, I sought
solace in the arms of my beloved, feeling her breath
trigger off my smothering passions once again

When I felt that the rotten stench of obnoxious vehicle
smoke virtually strangulating the last ounce of air
suspended in my lungs, I sought solace in a garden of
fragrant lotus, with the tingling odor adding a
perpetual smile to my face

When I felt that planet earth had become too claustrophobic to exist, with every single space jammed by hordes of people and machinery, I sought solace in the dark dungeons, where the slithering serpent captivated me wholesomely with its charm and dance

When I felt that the dust from the deserts was irascibly irritating my eyes, I sought solace in the heart of the ocean, where the frothy foam and fish entrenched me with insurmountable exhilaration

When I felt that scores of stinging mosquitoes from the city perilously intruded upon and spoilt my every night, I sought solace on the top of the mountain; where the air was pristine and fresh and where I was in talking distance with the stars

When I felt that the darkness of the satanic night was casting its evil spell upon me from all sides, I sought solace in the invincible lap of my mother

And when I felt that my faith in mankind was gradually dwindling, with an insatiable urge to flee this Universe forever burning high and handsome in my persona every second, I sought solace in front of the creator; kneeling in submissive stupor on his feet, to experience the rays of encouragement the omnipotent power to survive.

Dance upon every chance

Whether it be as inconspicuous as an invisibly
dissolute ant, or whether it be as towering as the
highest apogee of the invincibly towering mountain
upon which fell the very first rays of the brilliant Sun

Whether it be as overpoweringly black as the color of
unearthly midnight, or whether it be blazing towards
an infinite new civilizations of tomorrow—like the
profusely ameliorating beams of empowering dawn

Whether it be as evanescent as the parsimoniously
deteriorating horizons, or whether it be as veritably
fathomless as the gigantically swirling oceans and the
endless chain of black rocks

Whether it be as infantile as the nimble squeak of the
freshly born baby rat, or whether it be as impregnably
majestic as the inimitably unparalleled roar of the
unflinching lion

Whether it be as frivolous as the sporadically
changing winds, or whether it be as undefeatedly
passionate as the shades of insuperably humanitarian
and united blood

Whether it be as light-veined as the inane balderdash
of the limpid clown, or whether it be as redolently
immortalizing as a boundless line of ecstatically
bountiful poetry

Whether it be as acrimoniously arid as the blistering
sands, or whether it be as torrentially sumptuous and
everlastingly life-yielding as the unabashedly
tumbling droplets of golden rain

Whether it be as nonchalant as the ephemerally livid
whisper, or whether it be as royally unassailable as the
indefatigably euphoric and vociferous lightening of
the crimson sky

Whether it be as ludicrously feeble as the abnormally
rickety pack of cards, or whether it be as insuperably
fortified as the magical Universe whose foundations
rest on eternally unified love

Whether it be as excruciatingly tantalizing as the
betraying mirage, or whether it be as inevitably
definite as the perennially nurturing complexion of the
soil of a princely dark brown

Whether it be as nervously tottering as an abysmally
old man stumbling towards his grave, or whether it be
perpetually bouncing in the victorious vigor and ardor
of wondrously youthful life

Whether it be as dismally oblivious as the full cry of
the non-existent mosquito, or whether it be full,
eternal and ravishingly triumphant as the entire
Universe of philanthropic justice

Whether it be as disdainfully terrestrial as the transient
blade of pulverized green grass, or whether it
uninhibitedly flapped its wings like a surreally
adorned queen through fathomless bits of azure sky

Whether it be as cunningly slippery as the
bewilderingly groping eel, or whether it be as
infallibly faithful as the girl of your every dream, who
fearlessly stood abreast you to rejoice and smilingly
accept the ghastliest of death

Whether it be as uncannily eccentric as the croaking witch's anointed broomstick, or whether it be as enthrallingly pragmatic as the unnervingly ticking, centuries old town clock

Whether it be as deplorably jinxed as the fetidly disgruntled graveyard, or whether it be as miraculously blessed as every synergistically palpitating creation of the Omnipotent Almighty Lord

Whether it be as treacherously cheating like the feckless shadow which came and disappeared with each shade of the light, or whether it be as timelessly befriending as the breath in the lungs, which only left you after your veritable death

Whether it be as pathetically ungraspable as the stream of widowed water, or whether it be like all those people around you who unstoppably embraced you for solely what you were and what you were destined to be

And I really don't care. Be it in whatever shape, form, color or intensity; but as long as it is for the betterment of humanity and my very own self, the very instant it comes my way, I'll definitely and wholesomely DANCE UPON EVERY CHANCE.

Embrace unconquerable life

Suicide is a ghastily lingering spirit between
resplendently sparkling heaven and diabolically
ghastly hell

Suicide is the most desperately hedonistic crime
committed against every conceivable fraternity of all
mankind

Suicide is the most truculently unforgivable outburst
of any organism, murderously imperiling the crux of
symbiotically mesmerizing existence

Suicide is a ghoulishly amorphous abode, without the
most infinitesimal trace of doors windows and
robustly functioning entities

Suicide is an indescribably treacherous venom, which
brutally asphyxiates the impoverished ghost, even
after the wholesome end of priceless life

Suicide is the most preposterously scurrilous corpse
that incarcerated you from all sides, morbidly
dampening every quintessential iota of your blood

Suicide is the most luridly mortifying death that an
entity could ever undergo, ensuring that he
indefatigably suffocates in diminutive lid-fulls of
water, while the other world danced every time it was
born

Suicide is the most ultimate curse of the devil upon
every civilization, religion and tribe, afflicting the
fabric of society like an uncontrollably lambasting
tumor, which simply had no end

Suicide is perniciously sinister balderdash, the most incongruously distorted and heartlessly inclement fantasy that the stinking pigs could ever construe

Suicide is a coffin of disparagingly bludgeoning solitude, a measly quavering insect being blown away into the aisles of nothingness, at even the most mercurial draught of infidel wind

Suicide is a salaciously jinxed witch casting her spell of unsurpassable doom, even upon the most blissfully gratifying of destinies

Suicide is a vindictively hollow and lecherously gawky edifice, baselessly wavering towards the gallows of emptiness, without the most infinitesimal of foundations

Suicide is an inexplicably cancerous sorrow that gruesomely crucifies your soul, disdainfully maiming you on every step, for infinite more births of yours yet to unveil

Suicide is a flagrantly whipping extinction that had not the tiniest chance to ebulliently revive, stagnating in the prisons of torturously bleeding hell

Suicide is a chain of fanatically unpardonable misery, which perilously dries up every trace of mellifluously golden voice

Suicide is dreadfully sinful abnegating of breath without the Lord's consent, a misdeed which even his Omnisciently magnanimous grace could never ever condone

Suicide is a tunnel of blindness without any end

Suicide is the most punitive betrayal of truth, desire, dream and immortal love

Suicide is an unrelentingly bloodstained night which inconsolably cries

Therefore massacre the very thought, before it transcends you to commit forlorn suicide O! Man, and instead, embrace timeless sensuality, instead embrace enchanting beauty, instead embrace unconquerable life.

Life without a purpose

Life without a purpose is like a luxury liner
maneuvering wildly through the ocean without a
rudder

Life without a purpose is like a creeper growing up
tall without a brick wall for support

Life without a purpose is like an aircraft flying high in
the sky without a skilled captain

Life without a purpose is like an unruly classroom
without a learned teacher

Life without a purpose is like a drunk man traversing
through the streets hurling a volley of expletives

Life without a purpose is like a river flowing berserk
without side embankments

Life without a purpose is like an intricate necklace of
beads without a finely chiseled supporting wire

Life without a purpose is like a submissive population
reeling under the tyranny of dictatorship

Life without a purpose is like a crackling fire blazing
without enclosures to prevent it spreading

Life without a purpose is like a flamboyant car
without a steering wheel

Life without a purpose is like a stealthy spider
swirling around wildly in its web

Life without a purpose is like a stray dog growling for food mercilessly snatching the same from others of its kind

Life without a purpose is like mesmerizing rose growing on bountiful meadows, bereft of fragrance

Life without a purpose is like lovers courting each other without tying the sacrosanct threads of matrimony

Life without a purpose is like a lion gulping his food without scrupulously chewing

Life without a purpose is like the moon in the sky without scintillating shine

Life without a purpose is like a road of raw concrete without obstreperous traffic

Life without a purpose is like the most voluptuous of faces without a frivolous smile

Life without a purpose is like an intricately chiseled brain without an ocean of thoughts

Life without a purpose is like eating sumptuous food without relishing the same

Life without a purpose is like an inherited rich man without having the cognizance to spend his affluence

Life without a purpose is like breath inhaled in the body without being sensitively felt

Life without a purpose is like a palpable heart impregnated in the chest without having the capacity to throb

O yes! Life without a purpose is like living life
listlessly although being actually dead.

Lead life like a man

Drink like a rabbit, gently lapping at water cascading from white water springs of the mountain

Sleep like a demon, snoring thunderously without even moving a whisker at the most lethal of dynamite explosions

Perspire like a bull, slogging it hard under the steaming rays of the sun

Dance like a peacock, spreading your feathers to their full plumage under exotic outbursts of rain

Smile like a wild chimpanzee, baring your snow-white teeth without being the slightest overwhelmed by your surroundings

Run like a kangaroo, traversing the dense foliage of the jungle, taking ten strides at a time

Sing like the nightingale, inundating every barren spot in the vicinity with the ecstatic melody of your sound

Cry like a crocodile, shedding tears as gargantuan as the clouds on every area you tread

Sting like a scorpion, piercing supple and innocuous skin with the venomous poison in your fangs

Talk like a parrot, chattering incessantly as misty wisps of air and the aroma of delectable food strike you in their entirety

Roar like a lion, waking up every entity sleeping blissfully with a single growl of yours

Smell like the roots, emanating a voluptuously raw
odor just after the first spells of rain

Stand like an elephant, weathering each storm trying
to blow you with enviable ease

Dream like an angel, exploring the wildest regions
around the globe with rampant frenzy

Shiver like a goose, with infinite strands of hair
standing up in animation on the snow

Slaver like a dog, greedily protruding your tongue
panting passionately for water

Bathe like the dolphins, diving acrobatically into the
sapphire seas, your body engulfed completely by the
majestic waves

Chew like a cow, slowly munching your meals with
rejuvenated gusto

Scamper around like a squirrel, leaping friskily on the
myriad of dangling branches

Fly high like the eagles, flapping your wings
exuberantly with the cotton cocoon of clouds gliding
past your hair

Kick like a donkey, swinging your legs viciously
towards those who try to disturb your concentration

Lick like a cat, sucking every droplet of milk from the
steep-edged bowl

Yawn like the hippopotamus, candidly announcing
your desire to sleep even to mortals buried in their
corpses

Scream like the dinosaur, a single echo of yours
silencing all commotion in this world

Stare like the mammoth whale, making your opponent
blink a thousand times

Hear like a fox, detecting the most inconspicuous of
sounds, coming to know of your adversary, before it
actually commences to attack

Laze around like the tortoise, not bothering to poke
out your head even in the most scorching of sunlight

Shine like the stars, punctuating the eerie darkness of
night with your spellbinding glimmer

Burn like fulminating lava, igniting the most
lackluster of individuals with the ardor in your
flames

Dig like mice, making your burrow in loose mud at
lightening speeds

Hide like the reptile, evading all traces of light
existing in the Universe

Peck like the woodpecker, chiseling your way through
the most obdurate of wooden logs

Crawl like the spider, mystically weaving your way
across the strands of the flimsy web

Swish like a zebra, moving your tail to wave away the most minuscule of flies buzzing intermittently around your nose

Eat like a pig, greedily gobbling even the tiniest of toffee wrappers loitering on the road

Change color like a chameleon, adapting yourself furtively to virtually any surrounding you enter

Hunt like the vultures, hideously diving down and capsizing your prey

Be wise like the owl, prudently opening your eyes in the dark as well as stringent light

Care like the lioness, protecting your child from the faintest signs of evil lurking around

Enjoy like the otters, having a party of beans and raw wine well past after midnight

Explore like the panther, mercilessly paving your way through the remotest corner of the forest

Love like God, annihilating the word "discrimination" forever from your adulterated brain

And lead life like a man, wandering and discovering; struggling and romancing, dreaming and working to transform all your dreams as well as those of several around you into an immortal reality.

I simply don't want to waste my today

I don't remember the color of the shirt I was wearing
yesterday, the exact number of buttons adorning its
daintily frilled frontal periphery

I don't remember the roads which I frequented
yesterday, the routes which I travelled upon to reach
my destination in an absolute jiffy

I don't remember the faces I encountered yesterday,
the fascinating flurry of smiles which so gorgeously
made my wretched day

I don't remember the food I ate yesterday, the
stupendous delicacies which voraciously tickled
intricate cavities in my mouth

I don't remember the sleazy television serials I
witnessed yesterday, the comic people on the small
screen which made me uninhibitedly laugh, conjured
me to transit into a satisfied slumber

I don't remember the shops that I passed yesterday,
the resplendent festoon of gaudy lights and glow that
stole fractions of my moistened breath and air

I don't remember the time when I dozed yesterday, the
number of hours I slept in loud snores and perennial
peace

I don't remember the flavor of the tea I consumed
several times yesterday, the heavenly aroma that
imparted loads of ravishing warmth to my fatigued
demeanor

I don't remember the flowers which I smelt yesterday, feasting on the stupendous fragrance that wafted uncontrollably from their robust bodies

I don't remember the unprecedented cavalcade of exotic dreams which I conceived yesterday, the ingratiating state of tingling excitement into which they wholesomely rendered me

I don't remember the sounds which I profoundly heard yesterday, the supremely melodious tunes which took complete control of my impoverished body and soul

I don't remember the countless verses I embossed yesterday, the spell-binding tunes which I harnessed and composed with my very own thick blood

I don't remember the birds who perched on my window yesterday, the boisterous chirps which added insurmountable exuberance and ardor to my solitary life

I don't remember the birthday celebrations of my wife which were unveiled yesterday, the unfathomable pomp and gaiety which enveloped my dwelling from each conceivable side as the evening tranquilly descended

I don't remember the perfume which I applied yesterday, the alluring redolence which it wholesomely besieged me with at ethereal dawn

I don't remember the names of the people who amicably came to meet me yesterday, the marathon hours that I congenially conversed with the same to enlighten my wave of gloomy boredom

I don't remember the contemporary planes in which I
sat yesterday, the grandiloquently plush interiors, the
ornamental glass of ethnic silver in which I opulently
sipped red wine

I don't remember the signature I executed yesterday,
the flamboyant strokes I delectably chiseled with my
swanky pen on the face of the crisp cheque-book

And I don't even remember the unsurpassable
adulation, the fleet of prestigious accolades, which I
received yesterday, all the scintillating awards and
marvelous trophies which adorned my translucent
mantelpiece

For if I remembered my yesterday, drowning myself
in the glorious past which circumvented me
relentlessly in the past, then my fingers would
automatically refrain from work today

And basking in the glory of yesterday, I simply don't
want to spoil my fabulously rosy today.

I live to love

I don't eat to live. I live to eat tantalizing morsels of
exotic food, to placate insurmountable pangs of my
gluttony with the rudiments of captivating nature

I don't smell to live. I live to smell exotically redolent
and vivaciously blooming flowers, to dance with the
fairies on the summits kissing the Moon

I don't philander to live. I live to philander in the
aisles of untamed desire and perennially everlasting
fantasy

I don't admire to live. I live to admire all the
wonderfully philanthropic, the boundlessly
unsurpassable beauty lingering on this bountiful
planet

I don't sleep to live. I live to sleep, dream myself
unrelentingly into a land transcending paradise,
wholesomely oblivious to the uncouthly manipulative
vagaries besieging vicious mortals

I don't sweat to live. I live to sweat, persevering my
best under golden rays of the flamboyant Sun to caress
the ultimate crescendos of unparalleled success

I don't sing to live. I live to sing, stupendously
blending the tunes diffusing from my poignant throat
with the eternal bliss in the marvelous atmosphere

I don't blink to live. I live to blink, mischievously flirt
with nubile maidens, trespassing through a carpet of
ingratiating mysticism and incredulous enthrallment

I don't philosophize to live. I live to philosophize,
disseminating the perpetually harmonious essence of
truth and benevolent brotherhood to every cranny of
this Universe entrenched with inexplicable pain

I don't hear to live. I live to hear, profusely absorb the
most enamoring sounds in free space, to catapult
above the majestically heavenly clouds

I don't procreate to live. I live to procreate, spawn
countless of my kind, ensuring that I continue the
chapter of existence even after I abdicate my last iota
of breath

I don't race to live. I live to race, letting the spirit of
uninhibited exhilaration forever reign
supreme in each of my devastated senses, eternally
surging forward to rejoice at the awesomely
Omnipotent colors of life

I don't study to live. I live to study, indefatigably
endeavor to imbibe all the benign goodness entrapped
within the cocoons of invincible solidarity

I don't evolve to live. I live to evolve, blossoming into
an unfathomable festoon of newness as each instant
unveils, romanticizing in the full ardor of existence
until I quit my final breath

I don't adventure to live. I live to adventure, intrepidly
crusading over all impediments that confront me in
my way, plunging into a valley of unimaginable
exuberance even in the heart of precariously tingling
midnight

I don't write to live. I live to write, inundating fathomless volumes of ecstatically barren paper with exquisitely oligarchic fantasy and the epitome of literature

I don't breathe to live. I live to breathe, ignite thunderbolts of incomprehensible desire with each puff of air I exhale, supremely exult in the flames of compassionate sharing which life has to wholesomely offer me

And I don't love to live. I live to love, insatiably dedicating each of my heartbeats to the person I cherish, taking birth an infinite times more than infinity, to be born only as her lover, ever again.

I'll keep trying hard

I'll keep trying hard incessantly and till the time the
last iota of crimson blood incarcerated within my
poignant veins doesn't dry beyond the aisles of
infinitesimal nothingness

I'll keep trying hard relentlessly and till the time the
last bone down my tenaciously lanky spine doesn't
fatigue beyond the corridors of irrevocable
hopelessness

I'll keep trying hard indefatigably and till the time the
last line of destiny on my brazenly intrepid palms
doesn't abrade into the dormitories of wholesomely
bizarre extinction

I'll keep trying hard insatiably and till the time the last
muscle of my patriotically unassailable shoulders
doesn't blend completely with threadbare mud

I'll keep trying hard unrelentingly and till the time the
last hair of my overwhelmingly glistening scalp
doesn't wither into inconspicuous wisps of insipid
oblivion

I'll keep trying hard intransigently and till the time the
last tooth of my overwhelmingly formidable jaws
doesn't crumble into horrendously barbaric powder

I'll keep trying hard irrefutably and till the time the
last strand of my unflinchingly intrepid flesh doesn't
vanish into realms of horrific banishment

I'll keep trying hard intransigently and till the time the
last smile of my charismatically bountiful lips doesn't
stutter towards an inexplicably gory end

I'll keep trying hard tirelessly and till the time the last globule of empathy of my resplendently fearless eyes doesn't fully evaporate into ungainly tornados of nothingness

I'll keep trying hard incorrigibly and till the time the last blush of my robustly scarlet cheeks doesn't fade with the winds of obsoletely despicable dilapidation

I'll keep trying hard irretrievably and till the time the last iota of my piquantly galloping shadow doesn't juxtapose into worthlessly baseless dust with the treacherously ominous descent of sinister midnight

I'll keep trying hard euphorically and till the time the last whisper down my philanthropically scintillating throat doesn't stifle to a timidly capricious mellow, eventually transposing with dungeons of disdain

I'll keep trying hard unendingly and till the time the last morsel of enthusiasm in my vivaciously bouncing caricature doesn't inevitably snap into pernicious rivers of painstaking perspiration

I'll keep trying hard unconquerably and till the time the last speck of gloriously sparkling truth in my conscience doesn't assassinate into countless pieces of derogatorily pulverized ash

I'll keep trying hard unassailably and till the time the last millimeter of breath in my emphatically inhaling lungs doesn't drain out at the order of the Creator to perpetually abdicate life

And I'll keep trying hard immortally and till the time
the last beat of my passionately palpitating heart
doesn't succumb to the viciously malevolent
whirlpools of betrayal into the hands of the
barbarically pulverizing devil.

Every human is beautiful

Some had beautifully mesmerizing lips with a
voluptuously silken sheen enveloping their periphery

Some had astoundingly sharp eyes, able to sight
marathon distances even in the most obfuscated and
bleariest of light

Some had robust muscled legs, running for
astronomically long hours in the cold despite the
armory of barricades and odds

Some had exquisitely sculptured fingers, sketching
and evolving a fleet of shapes encompassing all
mankind

Some had tenaciously hard fists, which could drill a
hole through the acrid mountain, defend the country
against the salacious demon

Some had a stupendously sparkling complexion,
resembling the fairies and angels residing in the
omnipotent realms of heaven

Some had a delectably black color entrenching their
entire face, a shade of dark, impregnated in their
demeanor, which made them more enchanting than
every night

Some had a height as tall as the ceiling, walking with
profound authority and domination through the
verdant countryside

Some had a tongue which indefatigable spoke; sung;
whistled and chirped sweeter than the melodious
nightingale

Some had a stature shorter than a shrub, appearing like Moon Gods divinely trespassing on the body of this planet

Some had a memory as astonishing as the contemporary computer, deciphering mind-boggling sums of arithmetic with incredulous efficacy

Some had the remarkable talent to emulate any voice, entertaining people for countless decades with the overwhelming manipulation of their sound

Some had an insurmountably supreme command over vocabulary, spoke and wrote any language with ultimate command and grace

Some had the amazing ability to acrobatically leap in the air, juggle several balls for boundless seconds at a time

Some had the adroit skill of negotiation, were able to succeed in any professional venture of life which they decided to undertake

Some had the prowess to cook delicious morsels of enticing food, deluging the morbidly gloomy atmosphere with the aroma of freshly baked corn

Some had the art of imparting knowledge, taught and dexterously handled children of all ages in innocuous school

Some had the fiery flamboyance of the Sun, propelled the air jet at lightening speeds through vibrant carpets of floating air

Some had a passionately beating heart, which fell in
love the instant it witnessed the person of its dreams,
the person of its kind

Some had breath which ardently drifted down the
nostrils, ignited the still ambience in the vicinity,
triggering it with their unsurpassable intensity into a
fireball of vivacious flames

O yes! Every individual is a beautiful individual in
some respect or other, in some form or other, and I
have absolutely no inhibitions whatsoever in
disclosing, of course with the mutual consent of
Almighty God that every human is indeed beautiful.

Alive

If I perceived myself as a king, then I was indeed
perched on the embellished throne, with a festoon of
diamonds glittering royally by my side

If I perceived myself as a panther, then I was indeed
the menacing beast in the jungle, trampling rampantly
through the dense undergrowth, paving my own
inimitable way

If I perceived myself as a mountain, then I was indeed
the summit, shimmering magnificently under the
flamboyant rays of the sun

If I perceived myself as a peacock, then I was indeed a
pompous bird, blossoming my armory of vivacious
feathers ingratiatingly towards the sky

If I perceived myself as a beggar, then I was indeed
the ragamuffin spreading my hands abominably on the
streets, waiting for those indispensable coins of
currency to flood my scarred and impoverished hands

If I perceived myself as a duck, then I was indeed the
appeasingly dimpled monster, floating on the serene
surface of tepid water

If I perceived myself as an infinitesimal speck, then I
was indeed the diminutive mosquito, irascibly buzzing
around the divinely asleep eardrum

If I perceived myself as the fortified castle, then I was
indeed the invincible walls of iron which shrugged off
the mightiest of attacks with nonchalant ease

If I perceived myself as the grandiloquent sun, then I was indeed the fountain of mesmerizing rays which illuminated every cloistered cranny of earth

If I perceived myself as a criminal, then I was indeed the satanic hoodlum, intransigently bent upon devastating blissful mankind

If perceived myself as dumb, then I was indeed bereft of words and speech, standing like a retarded lunatic, when in fact I had a fathomless treasury of eloquence embedded in my soul

If I perceived myself as a magician, then I was indeed the astoundingly inexplicable conjurer, metamorphosing all chunks of bland mud into biscuits of gold

If I perceived myself as garbage, then I was indeed the pile of horrendously fetid sewage, lying dilapidated and decaying to rot

If I perceived myself as a cloud, then I was indeed a surreally fabulous fantasy, pelting down showers of flirtatious romance

If I perceived myself as a needle, then I was indeed the minuscule strand of metal disgustingly poking people in their ribs

If I perceived myself as darkness, then I was indeed a perpetually solitary ambience, enveloped from all sides by inevitably bizarre grief

If I perceived myself as sick, then I was indeed suffering from astronomically high fever, with my forehead blazing more than blistering embers of sizzling fire

If I perceived myself as happy, then I was indeed
exuberant, embracing the absolute pinnacle of
prosperity uninhibitedly with both arms

If I perceived myself as a shark, then I was indeed the
preposterously huge monster, ready to rip apart
innocuous personalities into infinite bits of their
original form

If I perceived myself as fearless, then I was indeed
valiantly doughty, ready to confront the most deadly
of catastrophes, without flinching or faltering the
slightest

If I perceived myself as a sheep, then I was indeed the
fleet-footed and daintily nimble animal, celestially
existing amongst boundless others of my kind

If I perceived myself as love, then I was indeed a
messiah profusely dedicated to propagating its
different forms far and distant across this colossal
Universe

If I perceived myself as hatred, then I was indeed
deceitful anecdotes of malice, snapping the cherished
essence of sacrosanct life

If I perceived myself as truth, then I was indeed an
irrefutable idol of honesty, assisting countless
individuals trapped in the dungeon of salacious
lechery, with optimism seeming an overwhelmingly
far cry away

If I perceived myself as ugly, then I was indeed the
unfortunate possessor of distorted features, with every
organ of my body gruesomely placed and repugnantly
grotesque

If I perceived myself as beautiful, then I was indeed gorgeous, with my lips portraying that voluptuously pink and robust tinge

If I perceived myself as unlucky, then I was indeed the man with a stone touch, converting each thing I caressed into rock hard boulder, when in fact the stars that shone on my birth were those befitting a prince

If I perceived myself as thunder, then I was indeed streaks of electric silver lightening ready to strike ground & tremendously terrorize

If I perceived myself as a candle, then I was indeed the uncertainly flickering flame, deluging the dreary ambience with a beam of vibrant hope and light

If I perceived myself as a pig, then I was indeed the incomprehensibly fat and greedy beast, ready to gobble virtually whatever I could lay my hands upon

If I perceived myself as a fruit, then I was indeed a rubicund sapling, ready to placate the gluttony of those who indispensably wanted food

If I perceived myself as a reflection, then I was indeed an ethereally appearing shadow, which cropped up in brightness and vanished completely with dolorously black light

If I perceived myself as a bone, then I was indeed a dreadful skeleton, with absolutely not the tiniest trace of energy left in my countenance

If I perceived myself as a smile, then I was indeed an entity wholesomely blended with joy, basking in the unprecedented glory of pure ecstasy

If I perceived myself as dead, then I was indeed buried
unfathomable feet beneath the soil, despite having my
heart palpitating violently beyond the boundaries of
life

And if I perceived myself as living, then I was indeed
having life, irrespective of the unsurpassable battalion
of hurdles that confronted me in my way, raring to
ubiquitously spread the wonderful essence of my
breath, raring to ubiquitously spread the most
sacred word of all, called ALIVE.

Five star

On the surface, it was merely a conglomerate of
meticulously assembled stone and colossal pillars,
extruding boundless feet from the trajectory of
congenially moist soil

But what made the castle stupendously FIVE STAR
was the majestic King, Queen and princess
philandering inside, the ambience of unconquerable
royalty that profusely perpetuated the air from all
sides

On the surface, it was an insipid amalgam of dry
twigs, streams, and fathomless kilometers of
insatiably untamed wilderness

But what made the forest irrefutably FIVE STAR was
the melodiously harmonious chirping of the spell-
binding nightingale, the poignantly enamoring trails of
the regally mischievous lion and kin

On the surface, it was a macabre view of countless
stray bones, agglutinated in articulate tandem and
disdainfully abhorring every sensitive entity around

But what made the brain omnisciently FIVE STAR
was its unsurpassable entrenchment of compassionate
fantasy, its unrelenting ability to conceive beyond
the realms of the infinite infinity

On the surface, they were just overwhelmingly lanky
poles of inconspicuously coagulated mud, pompously
protruding towards the mid-day sun

But what made the mountains invincibly FIVE STAR
was their unflinchingly intrepid ability to confront the
most acrimoniously mightiest of storms, uninhibitedly

sequestering one and all in swirls of gregarious belonging, handsomely alike

On the surface, it was just a flabbily gargantuan assemblage of foaming water, nervously rising and falling umpteenth times in a single minute, under the most evanescent rays of the sun

But what made the sea ravishingly FIVE STAR was its miraculously rejuvenating froth, the fountains of voluptuously tangy salt which it vibrantly diffused, after clashing against the seductive rocks

On the surface, it was just a frigidly sticky and pugnaciously dribbling liquid, shabbily corrupting all thoroughly synchronized space around

But what made the hive enchantingly FIVE STAR was its beautifully holistic scores of rambunctious bees, symbiotically mélangeing with the spirit of effusive existence, to disseminate ubiquitous sweetness all around

On the surface, it was just a parsimoniously molded cauldron of wax, obnoxiously infiltrating the blissful atmosphere with its snobbishly inflated stench

But what made the candle omnipresently FIVE STAR was its heavenly ability to illuminate even the most horrendously sinister darkness, impregnate a spell of optimistic enlightenment in the lives of those treacherously deprived

On the surface, it was just a ferocious-looking fireball of blistering gases, gruesomely charring even the most Herculean entity who dared to trespass by its belligerently flaming side

But what made the sun omnipresently FIVE STAR
was its rays of perpetually triumphant happiness, its
endless cradle of celestial light which unassailably
embraced every organism, irrespective of caste, creed,
or spurious rites

On the surface, he was just a haphazard
synchronization of flesh and bones, everything
savagely engulfed by unruly hair, hair and
capriciously mangled hair

But what made Man unchallengeably FIVE STAR
was the wave of Godly philanthropism in his
commiserating eyes, the apostle of Universal
benevolence wholeheartedly pouring from his amiable
palms

On the surface, it was just a disconcerting mass of
mucus and derogatory darkness, ghoulishly scaring
the wits of anybody who witnessed it for the very first
time

But what made the nostril omnipotently FIVE STAR
was its essence of timelessness, the tireless paradise of
air that it synergistically inhaled and exhaled to
astoundingly procreate the chapters of sacred survival

And on the surface, it was just a morbidly bubbling
river of blood and infinite nerves, thundering
uncertainly into the aisles of nothingness, as each
instant unveiled

But what made the heart perpetually FIVE STAR was
its exotically fascinating string of humanitarian beats,
immortalizing forever and ever the spirit of God's
most priceless gift called EXISTENCE.

Victory shall forever be

Every maelstrom of unendingly truculent misery was
whiplashed upon you by the hedonistic devil, as he
salaciously marauded with his fingers soaked in
innocent blood

God was irrefutably a beam of Omnipotent
righteousness, who not only blessed you with the
insurmountable power to conquer all evil, but created
infinite more of your kind tirelessly, every unfurling
minute of the night and day,

giving supreme liberty to the devil to do whatever he
could, in whatever form he could, but in the end he
would be pathetically decimated to inconspicuous ash
and victory shall forever be of unassailably majestic
truth,

Every corpse of ghoulishly ungainly torture and
invidiousness was thrust upon you by the parasitic
devil, as he indiscriminately trampled left, right, and
center, with brutally lascivious hunger lingering in his
eyes

God was irrefutably a sun of unconquerably princely
hope, who not only blessed you with the
unsurpassable power to behead all evil, but created
infinite more of your kind tirelessly every unfurling
minute of the night and day,

giving uninhibited liberty to the devil to do whatever
he can, in whatever form he can, but in the end he
would be transformed into wisps of insipid
nothingness, and victory shall forever be of invincibly
glorious truth

Every spirit of cadaverous desperation and malice was jinxed upon you by the savage devil, as he unsparingly plodded forward to devour all organisms alive

God was irrefutably the sky of fathomless beauty and ingratiating enchantment, who not only blessed you with the unflinching power to vanquish all evil, but created infinite more of your kind tirelessly every unfurling minute of the night and day,

giving unrestricted liberty to the devil to do whatever he can; in whatever form he can, but in the end he would crumble into disdainful oblivion, and victory shall forever be of altruistically patriotic truth

Every hell of preposterously raunchy sin and bawdiness was thrashed upon you by the hideous devil, as he dogmatically barked the tunes of abhorrently despicable lies

God was irrefutably a religion of symbiotically Omnipresent mankind, who not only blessed you with the peerless power to destroy all evil, but created infinite more of your kind tirelessly every unfurling minute of the night and day,

giving unparalleled liberty to the devil to do whatever he can, in whatever form he can, but in the end he would wholesomely reduce him into graveyards of parsimonious nothingness, and victory shall forever be of pristinely unblemished truth

Every whirlwind of indescribably penalizing lechery and sodomizing torment was slapped upon you by the devastating devil, as he insanely burnt till the last bone of his spine in the coffins of unrelenting hatred

God was irrefutably an omniscient harbinger of
everlasting peace, who not only blessed you with
inimitable fortitude to blow away all evil, but created
infinite more of your kind tirelessly every unfurling
minute of the night and day,

giving undaunted liberty to the devil to do whatever
he can, in whatever form he can, but in the end he
would be charred to inconsequential ash, and victory
shall forever be of gloriously immortal truth

Every speck of acrimoniously cancerous and
destructive disease was stabbed upon you by the
incarcerating devil, as he intransigently sulked in the
gallows of cold-bloodedly rotten death

God was irrefutably the priceless cosmos of
perpetually royal fructification, who not only blessed
you with the unchallengeable prowess to massacre all
evil, but created infinite more of your kind tirelessly
every unfurling minute of the night and day,

giving unstoppable liberty to the devil to do whatever
he can, in whatever form he can, but in the end he
would dissolve into the dustbins of extinction, and
victory shall forever be of blazingly impeccable truth

Every trace of orphaned wailing and hapless
loneliness was tainted upon you by the ignominious
devil, as he exhaled scorpions of remorseful prejudice
even in deep sleep

God was irrefutably a timelessly vivacious rainbow of
desire and fearless hope, who not only blessed you
with the insuperable ardor to finish all evil, but
created infinite more of your kind every unfurling
minute of the night and day,

Giving uncontrollable liberty to the devil to do whatever he can, in whatever form he can, but in the end he would lose every element of his existence, and victory shall forever be of the immaculately bountiful truth.

If I had closed my breath yesterday

If I had cut my fingers yesterday, how could I hold the scintillating cluster of diamonds strewn abundantly in the fields for me today?

If I had mercilessly chopped off my tongue yesterday, how could I call the names of the ones I cherish the most, the ones who are actually present before my eyes today?

If I had given my legs to the preposterously huge shark to swallow yesterday, how could I reach the summit of the gigantic mountain, which is just inches away from my body today?

If I had gruesomely blinded my eyes yesterday, then how could I admire and profoundly relish the mesmerizing sights which unveil in front of my eyes today?

If I had ruthlessly smashed my neck yesterday, how could I hoist it towards the Moon, which is shimmering in perennial bliss today?

If I had horrendously punctured both my ears yesterday, how could I profusely absorb all the enchanting sounds, which splendidly inundate the atmosphere today?

If I had apathetically sewed my lips together yesterday, how could I sing ingratiating songs for the person I love the most today?

If I had brutally pulverized all the bones in my ribs yesterday, how could I thunderously gyrate and swing to the tunes of animated nature today?

If I had insanely evacuated every droplet of blood from the veins in my body yesterday, how could I donate it to save the life of my mother, who is struggling for breath, and on the tenterhooks of extinction today?

If I had invidiously ripped apart even the last bit of my fingernails yesterday; how could I scratch at the heavenly chunks of cheese, insatiably caress the titillating couch of fur that engulfs me from all sides today?

If I had injected snake poison in my tender brain yesterday, how could I embrace the astronomical prowess of memory, the spellbinding ocean of imagination that awaits open-handed for me today?

If I had savagely dried the emphatic cloud of moisture from my jeweled eyeball yesterday, how could I ooze a river of exuberant tears for my separated ones, who met me after countless number of decades today?

If I had abruptly stopped my heart from beating yesterday, how could I worship the person who is irrefutably in love with me today?

And If I had strangulated my breath yesterday, forcing my being to relinquish life in utter frustration yesterday, how could I bask in the glory of the brilliant sun, which kisses my impoverished doorstep passionately today?

Young at heart

The leaves of the tree withered at the onset of autumn,
rendering it a bare and pathetic sight to witness,

although the body and trunk were still alive, they
screamed passionately as the wind slapped and
caressed them.

The most majestic of reptiles shed its skin while
undergoing a metamorphosis of seasons, partially
annihilating its grandeur,

although its slithering body still traversed in circuitous
routes and its fangs were ready to strike, injecting
lethal venom.

The mountain sheep had their wool sheared for
weaving thermal contrivances, leaving their
appearance shabbily disgraceful,

although they still wandered in harmony on the
colossal slopes, bleated in unison as dusk stealthily
approached.

The austere Sun God shed its brightness as nightfall
took over, resembling an insipid reflection of its
original identity,

although it still shone brilliantly the next morning,
illuminating stringently every bit of cloistered gloom.

The slender iron nail lost all its gloss as monsoon
showers poured incessantly from the sky, giving it a
deplorable appearance,

although it still maintained the capacity of being
embodied in the wall, and still had the hostility to
pierce an inflated balloon.

The fermented barrel of milk lay bereft of immaculate
white color, resembling worthless chunks of flaccid
curd,

although it still produced an extremely piquant taste,
had reasonably high levels of salubrious nutrition.

The flying birds shed infinite numbers of feathers
each day, looking bedraggled after being stripped of
their kingly plumage,

although they still retained the power to fly; soaring
high up in the air and procreating their progeny.

The banana after peeling its intricate skin appeared as
a dilapidated urchin, shivering uncontrollably in the
wind,

although it was sumptuous and relishing to eat, and its
pulp caused ravishing sensations in the buds of taste.

The biscuits of gold after losing their shine resembled
mundane coin, failed to captivate attention,

although they still had the same value, could fetch
their owners an astronomical fortune when judiciously
traded.

And all the old folks traversing the streets looked a
sight with which to sympathize profoundly, clinging
tightly to their walking sticks,

although they still had the power to love, the power to
overwhelmingly fantasize, as they were YOUNG
AND INNOCENT AT HEART.

Once again tomorrow

Yesterday was just a thing of the horrendously
treacherous past, fading and dissipating rapidly into
thin wisps of obsolete oblivion

Let's unite in strings of perpetual harmony and
compassion today, to blossom into a vibrantly
optimistic and spell-binding tomorrow

Yesterday was just a thing of the diabolically heinous
past, pathetically blending with insipid bits of raw ash

Let's unite in whirlpools of insurmountable solidarity
today, unflinchingly facing even the most acridly
mighty challenges, proudly sprouting into the blissful
civilizations of tomorrow

Yesterday was just a thing of the lecherously
abhorrent past, stinking like a million rats beneath the
dungeons of manipulative malice

Let's unite in irrefutable rings of truth today,
massacring every iota of horrifically despairing lies
and sadness, culminating into a wonderfully brilliant
tomorrow

Yesterday was just a thing of the remorsefully morbid
past, rapidly deteriorating to coalesce with the
murderous graves

Let's unite in clouds of celestial peace today,
indefatigably fantasizing above a land of enchanting
paradise, to give birth to a divinely non-violent
tomorrow

Yesterday was just a thing of the devastatingly evil
past; sinking into a sea of baseless nothingness to
mélange with the inconspicuously mundane sands

Let's unite in winds of uninhibited sharing today,
ubiquitously commiserating with shivering mankind
around us, to fulminate into a fountain of irrevocably
bestowing tomorrow

Yesterday was just a thing of the ominously ghastly
past, stabbing like a trillion malevolent dagger-heads,
before it eventually blew with the infinitesimally
capricious dust

Let's unite in tornados of untamed passion today,
incinerating flames of overwhelming desire even in
the most frozen of waters, to majestically bloom into a
intrepidly flamboyant tomorrow

Yesterday was just a thing of the savagely decaying
past, perpetuating its deplorably surreptitious shadow
into the fabric of the blissful society, before it finally
withered into a corpse of absolute submission

Let's unite under skies of philanthropic benevolence
today, endeavoring our very best to alleviate
debilitatingly deprived society, escalating exuberantly
into an Omnipotently egalitarian tomorrow

Yesterday was just a thing of the insidiously remote
past, ludicrously baring its meaningless fangs before it
wholesomely lost every iota of its voice

Let's unite in the religion of humanity today, to
unequivocally disseminate the immortal virtue of
mankind, dazzle into a bountifully royal tomorrow

And yesterday was just a thing of the tragically
shattered past, profusely betraying light and hope,
before it was ferociously punished and sent to the
island of satanic hell

Let's unite in beats of immortal love today, embracing
one and all irrespective of caste, creed, or color, alike,

to sway forever in the corridors of marvelous heaven,
every time the Creator wants us to be born once again
tomorrow.

Please smile

A smile on your lips comes absolutely free, spreading waves of unsolicited exhilaration in my person

A smile on your lips looks mystically enchanting, resembling sweet coats of molten nectar

A smile on your lips accentuates your immaculate teeth, portraying your mesmerizing grace

A smile on your lips gives me loads of renewed hope, instantly assassinating all the anguish I face

A smile on your lips reveals your boisterous nature, encompassing me completely in supreme exultation

A smile on your lips impregnates me with hope, prompting me to overcome a battalion of dismal failures

A smile on your lips makes me walk fast, keep up pace with the uncouth speed of mundane world

A smile on your lips looks ravishing in the tenacious moonlight, instigating me to stare unrelentingly in your sapphire eyes

A smile on your lips sculptures your face to resemble a fairy, bestowing upon my dreary soul a plethora of riches

A smile on your lips makes me oblivious to time, and hours unleash themselves into days without traces of boredom

A smile on your lips reinvigorates my exhausted
bones, encouraging me to walk
for marathon distances in the sweltering heat of the
sun

A smile on your lips makes me feel exorbitantly
special, placing me several shades above the common
pedestrian

A smile on your lips makes me ostentatiously dream,
sequestering me from harsh realities, blending me
with the ostentatious walls of the palace

A smile on your lips incorporates me with tumultuous
confidence, making me speak extravagantly at
business meetings

A smile on your lips gives you that frivolous look,
melting my stringently compact composure, instilling
my demeanor with inevitable desires

A smile on your lips makes me feel I am flying high in
thin clouds, incessantly constructing a building of
dreams

A smile on your lips reinstates my belief in mankind,
inducing me to be philanthropic towards my fellow
beings

A smile on your lips pacifies soaring temperatures of
viral fever in my silhouette, alleviating the soreness in
my intricate throat

A smile on your lips makes me incorrigibly feel I am
real, have a definite purpose while existing on this
earth

A smile on your lips distinguishes you from the solitary girl, granting you the invincible status of being holistically alive

So for heaven's sake, sweetheart, wake up from the realms of unconsciousness and
PLEASE SMILE!

Without the slightest fear

When I sat under the fulminating beams of the Sun, I felt an insatiable urge in my body to leap in untamed exhilaration and dance

When I sat in front of the scintillating mirror, I felt like candidly analyzing even the most minuscule part of my person

When I sat beside the enchantingly serene riverside, I felt like nostalgically reminiscing the innocuous flurry of moments which had wholesomely enveloped my childhood

When I sat by the profusely foliated tree, I felt like bouncing up and down like the vivacious squirrels, wistfully awaiting for the succulent fruits to harmoniously pour down on my famished belly

When I sat under the conglomerate of voluptuously exotic clouds, I felt like wandering with the heavenly fairies, fantasizing my mind to the most unprecedented limits

When I sat on the stern of the grandiloquent ship, I felt younger than a wailing child, with the exuberant waves of the ocean impregnating Herculean loads of rejuvenating energy in my dreary bones

When I sat on a blanket of chilly snow, I felt numbing arrows of death stabbing me from all sides, the scarlet blood running robustly through my veins, freezing into rosy ice-cream

When I sat on the panthers back, I felt for a moment to be the king of the jungle, although I had my heart in my bootlaces after a while had elapsed, and the beast snarled ferociously to its heart's content

When I sat abreast a hive of swarming bees, I fantastically felt the cocoons of golden honey sandwiched handsomely in the pockets, however was soon transported several feet beneath my coffin, as the maiden Queen kissed me nimbly on my nose

When I sat near the dolorously morbid grave, I felt tears of inexplicable agony well up my eyes, an uncanny wave of fear slowly engulf my blissful soul

When I sat on a battalion of menacing crocodiles, I felt overwhelmingly excruciating pangs of pain as the monsters ripped me apart till the last bone down my spine

When I sat on the century-old vacant throne, I felt like a majestically embellished royal prince, having been given the supreme reigns in my hands to rule the township once again

When I sat amidst an army of pot-bellied tortoise, I felt whirlpools of laziness circumvent my demeanor, an inexorable urge in my body to sleep in contentment till times immemorial

When I sat on the splendidly striped dolphins, I felt like swirling in full fervor of boisterous life, rolling my visage in tumultuous frenzy with the splashing water

When I sat on the summit of the astronomically towering mountain, I felt the entire world was a box of insipid matchsticks, drank air into my lungs like a man inhaling his last breath

When I sat at whisker lengths from my beloved, I felt infernos of invincible passion entrench my countenance, an irrefutable longing in my lips to caress her rubicund cheeks

When I sat in front of the Creator's idol, I felt blessed in every single respect of existing life, emerged victorious from behind my vicious cloudburst of gloom, to spread the true essence of happiness

But it was only when I sat close to my mother, that I felt I was the strongest man on this earth, divulging to her whatever circulated in the innermost compartments of my heart

and it was here that my world came to an abrupt end, and it was here that I discovered my true identity, and it was here that I slept immortally without the slightest fear.

Advance Comment

These 44 poems revolve around the polemical piece "Stop feeling sorry," which turns on a version of Frankl's existential solution to the problem of meaning, that is via second order "freedom of attitude." In *Seeking Solace*, Nikhil Parekh makes a virtue of embracing—of accepting; of affirming— all "celestial living kind." His exultant speaker embraces Romantic flourish, unironically trumpeting lines like "LIFE is BEAUTIFUL" and "this chapter called LIFE." The collection is an embodied celebration of the syllable. The speaker, at once innocent and wise, crowds every line with logorrhoea, with words words words, as though commanded from on high. Nikhil Parekh's speaker also exhorts his listeners to espouse words, that is, to take solace in the sensual experience of listening.

Jason S Polley
Associate Professor, Department of English Language and Literature, Hong Kong Baptist University
Jason S Polley, Wing Kin Vinton Poon, and Lian-Hee Wee (eds). *Cultural Conflict in Hong Kong: Angles on a Coherent Imaginary*. Palgrave, 2018.

SOME POETRY AND POETRY COLLECTIONS
Published by Proverse Hong Kong

A Gateway Has Opened, by Liam Blackford. 2021.

Alphabet, by Andrew S. Guthrie. 2015.

Astra and Sebastian, by L.W. Illsley. 2011.

Black Holes Within Us (translation from Macedonian),
by Marta Markoska. 2021

Bliss of Bewilderment, by Birgit Bunzel Linder. 2017.

The Burning Lake, by Jonathan Locke Hart. 2016.

Celestial Promise, by Hayley Ann Solomon. 2017.

Chasing light, by Patricia Glinton Meicholas. 2013.

China suite and other poems, by Gillian Bickley. 2009.

Entanglements:Physics, love, and wilderness dreams,
by Jack Mayer, 2022 (Scheduled)

Epochal Reckonings, by J.P. Linstroth. 2020.

For the record and other poems of Hong Kong,
by Gillian Bickley. 2003.

Frida Kahlo's cry and other poems,
by Laura Solomon. 2015.

Grandfather's Robin, by Gillian Bickley. 2020.

Heart to Heart: Poems, by Patty Ho. 2010.

H/ERO/T/IC BOOK (translation from Macedonian),
by Marta Markoska. 2020.

Home, away, elsewhere, by Vaughan Rapatahana. 2011.

Hong Kong Growing Pains, by Jon Ng. 2020.

Immortelle and bhandaaraa poems,
        by Lelawattee Manoo-Rahming. 2011.

In vitro, by Laura Solomon. 2nd ed. 2014.

Irreverent poems for pretentious people,
        by Henrik Hoeg. 2016.

The layers between (essays and poems),
        by Celia Claase. 2015.

Of leaves & ashes, by Patty Ho. 2016.

Life Lines, by Shahilla Shariff. 2011.

Moving house and other poems from Hong Kong,
        by Gillian Bickley. 2005.

Over the Years: Selected Collected Poems, 1972-2015,
        by Gillian Bickley. 2017.

Painting the borrowed house: poems,
        by Kate Rogers. 2008.

Perceptions, by Gillian Bickley. 2012.

Please Stand Back from the Platform Door,
        by Vishal Nanda. 2021.

Poems from the Wilderness, by Jack Mayer. 2020.

Rain on the pacific coast, by Elbert Siu Ping Lee. 2013.

refrain, by Jason S. Polley. 2010.

Savage Charm, by Ahmed Elbeshlawy. 2019.

Shadow play, by James Norcliffe. 2012.

Shadows in deferment, by Birgit Bunzel Linder. 2013.

Shifting sands, by Deepa Vanjani. 2016.

Sightings: a collection of poetry, with an essay,
'Communicating Poems', by Gillian Bickley. 2007.

Smoked pearl: poems of Hong Kong and beyond,
        by Akin Jeje (Akinsola Olufemi Jeje). 2010.

Of symbols misused, by Mary-Jane Newton. 2011.

The Hummingbird Sometimes Flies Backwards,
        by D.J. Hamilton. 2019.

The Year of the Apparitions,
        by José Manuel Sevilla. 2020.

Twilight Language,
        by Vinita Agrawal, 2022 (Scheduled).

Uncharted Waters, by Paola Caronni, 2021.

Unlocking, by Mary-Jane Newton. March 2014.

Violet, by Carolina Ilica. March 2019.

Wonder, lust & itchy feet, by Sally Dellow. 2011.

POETRY ANTHOLOGIES
Published by Proverse Hong Kong

Mingled voices: the international Proverse Poetry Prize anthology 2016,
    edited by Gillian and Verner Bickley. 2017.

Mingled voices 2: the international Proverse Poetry Prize anthology 2017,
    edited by Gillian and Verner Bickley. 2018.

Mingled voices 3: the international Proverse Poetry Prize anthology 2018,
    edited by Gillian and Verner Bickley. 2019.

Mingled voices 4: the international Proverse Poetry Prize anthology 2019,
    edited by Gillian and Verner Bickley. 2020.

Mingled voices 5: the international Proverse Poetry Prize anthology 2020,
    edited by Gillian and Verner Bickley. 2021.

Mingled voices 6: the international Proverse Poetry Prize anthology 2021,
    edited by Gillian and Verner Bickley. 2022.

FIND OUT MORE ABOUT PROVERSE AUTHORS, BOOKS, EVENTS AND LITERARY PRIZES

Web: <http://www.proversepublishing.com>
Our distributor's website:
<https://cup.cuhk.edu.hk/Proversehk>
twitter.com/Proversebooks
www.facebook.com/ProversePress

Request our free E-Newsletter
Send your request to info@proversepublishing.com.

Availability
Available in Hong Kong and world-wide
from our Hong Kong based distributor,
the Chinese University of Hong Kong Press,
The Chinese University of Hong Kong, Shatin, NT,
Hong Kong SAR, China.
See the Proverse page on the CUHKP website:
<https://cup.cuhk.edu.hk/Proversehk>

All titles are available from Proverse Hong Kong,
http://www.proversepublishing.com

Most titles can be ordered online from amazon
(various countries).

Stock-holding retailers
Hong Kong (CUHKP, Bookazine)
England (Ivybridge Bookshop)
Canada (Elizabeth Campbell Books)
Andorra (Llibreria La Puça, La Llibreria).

Also, orders may be made from bookshops
in the UK and elsewhere.

Ebooks
Most of our titles are available also as Ebooks.

Made in the USA
Columbia, SC
19 October 2022

69700742R00088